"If we cannot yet love one another,
then in God's name let us not hate each other too much."

**Rodrigo Roa Duterte
16th President of the Philippines**

One Anothering Volume One
By Marvin A. Marcelino
2021 All Rights Reserved.

Cover Design by Marvin Marcelino

Image credits to:
http://weheartit.com/entry/20491385/via/Eleladyvanity
http://mumuandsqueaksplace.blogspot.com/2013/07/funny-finger-faces-wallpapers.html
http://josephw390.deviantart.com/art/Finger-People-Best-Friends-For-Life-286123627
http://www.pakistantribe.com/wp-content/uploads/2014/04/Smile-6.jpg

Scriptures are from
The Holy Bible: King James Version, copyright 1611 used by permission of Collins World.
The Holy Bible: Revised Standard Version copyright 1901 by American Bible Society. Used by permission.
The Holy Bible New International Version, Copyright 1984 by International Bible Society. Used by permission.

ISBN:
Hardbound-978-621-470-009-7
Mobile/Kindle-978-621-470-010-3
Softbound/Paperback-978-621-470-011-0

Published by;
Poetry Planet Book Publishing House
688 Rosario Pozorrubio, Pangasinan 2435 Philippines
Contact Number: 09554960044
Email: maritesritumalta@gmail.com

Marvin Marcelino

One Anothering

VOLUME ONE

MARVIN A. MARCELINO

Blessed is the influence of one
true loving soul on another.
VICTOR HUGO

DEDICATED TO
Joshua Marvin my First-born
Mayumi Jasmine the Apple- of-my-eye
Mark Jiro the Seed of Love
Jasmin, my wife, and Inspiration

Marvin Marcelino

Acknowledgments

As I write these words of acknowledgements, much time passed since I began writing *One Anothering* way back in 1998.

There are many people to thank for their support and encouragement.

To the young people of that small church in Puting-kahoy Silang, Cavite, who listened to my lecture about conflict resolution. That small lecture grew into this full-grown book.

To all people who contributed through their unconscious slips-up which are noteworthy for a study.

To the many lovely people who gave several suggestions and improvements to the manuscript.

Thanks to all my friends who gave me a tap on my shoulder and believed in this work.

Jasmin my wife also serves as my *love-technical-supervisor.*' My three children: Joshua, Mayumi, and Jiro, they serve as my *assistants,* for revealing the fruits of love and labor.

I thank God the most for loving me no matter what I am and for His help in dealing with my being unloving, which have plagued my life. I am truly grateful to God for the love I found in Him.

Marvin Marcelino
Thailand

Perhaps they were right in putting love into books...
Perhaps it could not live anywhere else.
WILLIAM FAULKNER

The fact that we all need and crave for love,
and so little of it could be seen around.
LEO BUSCAGLIA

Marvin Marcelino

Preface

This book is a product of love. In my years of serving young people, two reasons came up for this book. One is that in any group of people, whether old or young, conflict is always a present potential threat. Why at times a person cannot simply get along with another? Conflict is a vicious cycle that, if ignored, is a deadly trap. Secondly, youth and church leaders and even co-workers need guide materials to address their groups in conflict.

The people and situations I observed while writing was helpful in getting some insights. Indeed, the people who have most contributed to completing this book are the people in conflict. The design of this book is to address the need of materials for personal growth, devotional, and small group activities for interpersonal relations. This is excellent for home, school, church, and the workplaces.

It is a *guidebook* for Christian social relations. It will help you polish your interpersonal relationships with one another.

It is a *devotional book,* which you can use to strengthen your spiritual life.

It is an *excellent activity book* for young and old, excellent for small group activities. This book will surely improve your small group members' relationships.

It is a *reference book* for short talks or sermons. You can even use this as a series for the week of prayer or family relation seminars for the whole year and a textbook for Values class.

It is a *family book*; you could use to and iron out differences at home, church, and workplace.

I hope this book addresses your intrapersonal and interpersonal relation needs. May the result be as what Virgil, the philosopher once said, "**Nunc scio quit sit amor**" (Latin) "Now I know what love is".

Where there is love there is life
MAHATMA GANDHI

Love is life. And if you miss love, you miss life.
LEO BUSCAGLIA

Marvin Marcelino

How to use this book

There are two ways to use this book.

For Personal Use

Use it as a devotional or study book.

The Activity part has questions that are too personal to be made public. You can keep it or share at your disposal.

For Group Use

Follow these six steps for group study.

Step one: As an opener, do the *Confront* section as instructed, best if each participant own a copy of this book to answer.

Step two: Proceed to the *Confer: Guide Questions for Discussion.* This will serve as an ‹ice breaker› for group dynamics. This is best when a facilitator guides the discussions. Try to come up with different views and deal with the pros and cons of the topic at hand.

Step three: Read the *Consider* section loud to the group to gain some insights. You can expand, as long as you do not go away from the essence.

Step four: Commit section, share tips on "how to". This is best if each participant has a Bible to read and to mark.

Step five: Do the Prayer individually or by groups (twos, three or more), especially pray with people whom you are in conflict. The prayer is an avenue to clear out individual differences.

Step six: Let everybody recite the Affirmation part aloud. Affirmation statements will help you wrap up the discussion by summarizing the principles learned and pledge to keep it.

I do hope you enjoy ***One Anothering***!

Contents

Marvin Marcelino

The ultimate lesson all of us have to learn
is unconditional love, which includes not only others
but ourselves as well.
ELISABETH KUBLER-ROSS

I hate and I love. Perhaps you ask why I do so.
I do not know but I feel it, and I am in torment.
CATULLUS

Introduction

Are you looking for love? Are you looking for the sense of being loved? Do you feel the coldness of people around you? Are you in search of ways to give others steps to teach them to love? Are you wanting to grow in love and relationship? Do you want to understand the deeper root cause of conflict and suggest repairs for everybody to live harmoniously with each other?

One Anothering deals with how to relate with another person according to the Word of God. This book answers two basic questions. First, what does it really mean to love one another? Second, how can one really love another? In the process, we will use the Bible to tell us how to relate with other people. This book intends not to define love, for many authors and books have done that. Many people seek the help of experts, scholars, scientists, social workers, psychologists, clergymen, politician even self-professed prophets to give solutions to this conflict-riddled world, yet I think we have been missing the basics of how human should relate to one another.

Christ Jesus has said, "Iniquities shall abound and the love of many shall be wax cold." (Matthew 24:12) The prophecy posed as a seemingly insoluble future problem. Christ had already given the solution to the problem of chaos, of conflicts and of misunderstandings. Jesus did not only say that we should love one another, but He demonstrated how to love another.

One day, God spoke to a man who had been praying for a better world. God said, "Your task is to build a better world." "How?" the man questioned, "the world is vast and complicated. There is nothing I can do." God with all wisdom simply said, "Build a better you in Christ Jesus." Why do we need to improve ourselves with Jesus? Remember that without Jesus we cannot do anything (John 15:5).

A famous writer Ellen G. White set the alarm that, "the need of union with Christ and with one another is our only safety in these last days. Let us not make it possible for Satan to point to our church members saying, "Behold how these people standing under the banner of Christ hate one another?"1

Our objective is to rediscover the practicality of loving one another; a godly love in action. Let us rediscover the *how to* of loving others and using the Holy Bible as our guide. What do we live for is not to make life difficult for each other. We have come to this world not to be loved, but to love, not to get but to give and not to be served but to serve.

"As long as we are in the world, we must link with one another. Humanity is interlaced and interwoven with humanity, as Christians we are members one of another. The Lord has made us thus, and when disappointments come, we are not to think worse of one another. We are individual members of a whole body. In helplessness and disappointments, we are fighting the battle of life. Moreover, God has designed us as His sons and daughters, whom He calls His friends to help one another. This is to be part of our practical Christian work."2

We are living in the era where individualism has matured. We are living as people afflicted with the *kanya-kanya* (to each his own) syndrome and we are all infected. Only the Great Healer can remove a contagious disease from our body, a disease that is never designed and accepted in the place He is preparing for us (John 14:1-3).

The Author and Finisher of our faith (Hebrews12: 2) has given the instruction for us to follow and has shown us the *how to* of ***One Anothering***. God gave us the manual, which we call the Bible. God is determined to make us worthy enough to be in heaven. This book is not the panacea to spiritual diseases but a tool to help each of us to have a better relationship with one another. As Ellen White

Marvin Marcelino

confirmed, "Only love can love be awakened." Ralph Waldo Emerson adds, "All mankind loves a lover."

Grace Goudhue Coolidge averred, "Love was not given to the human heart for careless dealings; its spark was given that man might know the divine revealing." "Take heed lest ye forget and be over task by the cares of this present world" (Luke 21:34). "Love is indeed heaven upon the earth," preached William Penn, "since heaven above would not be heaven without it."

Petrach taught, "Love is the crowning grace of humanity, the holiest right of the soul, the golden links which binds us to duty and truth, the redeeming principle that chiefly reconciles the heart of life and in prophetic of eternal good." Benjamin Disraeli agrees, "We are all born for love; it is the principle of existence and its only end." Like Paul's vision "If it be possible as many lives in you, live peaceably with all men" (Roman 12:18).

When I understand myself, I understand you,
and out of that understanding comes love.
JIDDU KRISHNAMURTI

Our survival seems to depend upon our relationship.
In childhood, if we are denied
of love encounters with humans, as a result,
we wither, fall into psychosis, idiocy or die.
LEO BUSCAGLIA

Doing What I Do
Not Want To Do

CONFRONT:

TO DO OR NOT TO DO List the things you like to do but...

1. What I know is good, but I do not do.

_______________________   _______________________

2. What I know is wrong, but I do.

_______________________   _______________________

3. What God wants me to do that I never do.

_______________________   _______________________

4. What I do that God hates?

_______________________   _______________________

CONFER: Guide questions for discussion

1.   Have you experienced doing unrighteous acts? How did you feel during and after committing the immoral deed?

2.   What reasons can you think of why we have the tendency to do what is morally wrong?

3.   Should we blame our parents for the wrong deeds we do?

4.   Was Dorothy Nolte's observation true about how children learn? Share your experience.

5.   Why is it necessary for us to understand the dilemma Paul experienced in Romans 7:15?

Doing What I Do
Not Want To Do

I do not understand what I do…
But what I hate to do I do. Romans 7:15 NIV

"I do not know why I just did what I did!" answered one student. Why do we commit sin? A question I threw at my Values class. Scary is not it? Another student raised her hand and said, "We find it okay because others were doing it too." I threw my next question. "Does anyone know that it is inappropriate to commit sin? "No sir!" One young man stood up and bluntly said, "We are naturally conditioned to do wrong."

'Naturally conditioned?' Therefore, can we say then that conflict, misunderstandings and fighting are but natural? Is it not this habit an incomprehensible by-product of sin? Apostle Paul was right in his observation about this sinning habit in us.

Horace Mann illustrated when he said, "Habit is like a cable, we weave a thread of it every day, and at last, we cannot break it." Samuel Johnson adds, "For the chains of habit are generally too small to be felt until they are too strong to be broken." John Dryden concludes, "We first make our habits then our habits form us."

Daniel Webster was right when he said, "Sow a thought, and reap an act. Sow an act reap a habit. Sow a habit reap a character. Sow a character reap a destiny. This sowing of small habits makes our senses numb and makes us think that the wrongs we do are always right. In conflict, we see ourselves always right and others are not. However, Charles Spurgeon, a champion preacher urged us to, "beware of no one more than yourself, for we carry our worst enemy everywhere within us." You see, there are so many habits, and they are mostly bad.

Marvin Marcelino

Who's to be blamed?

Read Dorothy L Nolte's poem *Children Learn What They Live*, traces from this observation, and reflect on your childhood experience.

Children Learn What They Live3
*Dorothy L. Nolte*If

If the children live with critics,
they learn to condemn.
If the children live with hostility,
they learn how to fight.
If the children live with fear,
they learn to be apprehensive.
If the children live with pity,
they learn to feel sorry for themselves.
If the children live with ridicule
they learn to be shy.
If the children live with jealousy,
they learn what envy is.
If the children live with tolerance,
they learn to be patient.
If the children live with encouragement,
they learn to be confident.
If the children live with praise,
they learn to appreciate.
If the children live approval,
they learn to like themselves.
If the children live with acceptance,
they learn to find love in the world.
If the children live with recognition,
they learn to have goal.
If the children live with sharing,
they learn to be generous.
If the children live in with honesty and fairness,
they learn what truth and justice are.
If the children live with friendliness,
they learn that the world is a nice place to be with
If the children live with serenity,
they learn to have peace of mind.

Let us go back in time through these questions. What type of home life did you have? What childhood living have you experienced? What environment did you grow up in? Was your environment pleasant or conflict free? Should we blame our parents, for the unpleasant traits we acquired from them?

Ellen G White the famous writer wrote, "Character building is the most important work ever entrusted to man."4 Eleanor Roosevelt lectured, "Character building begins at infancy and continues until our death." Everybody indeed has an enormous responsibility in the development of the character of another, and at times the most neglected responsibility of man in all walks-of-life. We have individual homework to do. We cannot remain ignorant of certain principles and guidelines that prevent us from being a slave of the inappropriate habits.

Why can I not do the right?

Why I cannot do, what I know is right? The same question Apostle Paul asked himself. "Why cannot I do right? Yet, I find myself doing the things I hate doing" (Romans 7:15). He found the reason: "For all have fallen short of the glory of God, all has sinned" (Romans 3:23), also "no one is righteous not one" (Romans 3:10). Whatever right we do our way we cannot win this sinning habit in us because our "heart is deceitful, and no man can understand it" (Jeremiah 17:9). Okay, so I want this sinful man overhauled. When do I start? The question is not when, but where.

How to overcome the unhealthy habits we have grown up with may seem like a hopeless case. We are all defeated by sin and becoming good seems impossible. Guaranteed, we can still overcome sin; by the sufficient grace, God gives us daily. (Ephesians 2:1-10).

Where do I Start?

Start with your heart! Seneca, a philosopher said, "The victory over oneself is of all victories the first and the first, and to master self is the greatest mastery." Let us examine our heart for it is deceitful (Jeremiah 17:10). Repent and confess to God to forgive us. Yes, God is just to forgive us our sins and purify us from our unrighteousness (disgusting habits) (1John1:9). For Jesus said, "Without Me, you cannot do anything" (John 15:5). For in Him you are a new creation the old is deleted (2Corinthians 5:17). In addition, God will cleanse one from all his impurities, and all his cherished impurities. He will give a new heart and put in a new spirit. He will remove the heart of stone, and give a heart of flesh, and then He will put the Holy Spirit in you and will move you to follow, do and keep His laws (Ezekiel 36:25-27). What is the character of a new person? Here is what the spirit of Prophecy says, "A new person will know that Love is the law of life for earth and heaven."5 "When God has the rightful place on the throne of the heart, the right place is for our neighbor. We shall love him as ourselves, and only as we love God supremely is it possible to love our neighbor impartially."6 "In the heart revered by divine grace, love is the principle of action; it modifies the character, governs the impulses, controls the passions, subdues enmity, and ennobles the affections."7

Benjamin Franklin suggested, "One vicious habit rooted out each year, in time make the worst man good." Reformation is what makes a man good. Once said, "Reformation like charity must begin at home." Samuel Johnson wrote, "Once we're all home it will radiate outward, possibly into all that we touch and work, ever kindling new light everywhere spreading in geometric ratio, far and wide doing only good wherever it spreads not evil." An adage says, "If we work upon marble, it will perish. If we work upon bronze, time will affect it. If we build temples, they will crumble into dust. But if we work upon immortal souls, if we imbue them with just principles of action with fear for wrong and love of right, we engrave on a true table stone, something which no time can destroy, which will brighten through all eternity." That is character building for heaven!

HOW TO AVOID THE WRONG
I ALWAYS DO

- ❑ Fear God (Ecclesiastes 12:13).
- ❑ Be clean of filthiness (2Cortinthians 7:1).
- ❑ Be spotless (2Peter 3:14).
- ❑ Be blameless (Ephesians 1:4).
- ❑ Be holy (Colossian 3:12).
- ❑ Ask God for wisdom (James 1:5,6).
- ❑ Follow Jesus' steps (1Peter 2:21, 22).
- ❑ Know what God hates. (Proverbs 16:5)
- ❑ Live Godly in Christ Jesus (2Timothy 3:12).
- ❑ Do the will of God from the heart (Ephesians 6:6).
- ❑ Live in the Spirit (Galatians 5:25).
- ❑ Let Christ live in you (Galatians 2:20).
- ❑ Live by the power of God (2Corinthians 13:4).
- ❑ Remember you are a child of light, not of darkness (1Thessalonians 5:5).

PRAYER

Dear Heavenly Father, I confess that I have found myself doing unrighteous deeds. Help me Father to overcome this weakness of doing ___________. I beg the Holy Spirit to direct my path to righteous deeds, to do only the will of God. Father, keep me blameless, spotless that I may glorify Your name. This I pray in the name of Jesus Christ, my Lord and Savior. Amen.

AFFIRMATION

I am now a new creation in Christ Jesus. Everything I do is only by the will of God and for His glory.

Marvin Marcelino

God has given us enough wisdom to make
improvements in our relation.
MIKHAIL GORBACHEV

Love is your continual guide towards
the highest level of consciousness
of which man is capable.
LEO BUSCAGLIA

The Rule of Psychological Reciprocity

WATYAGIB IS WATYAGET
Fill in the blanks.

1. How do you wish others would treat you?

____

____

____

____

2. What have you done for others that you would like done to you?

____

____

____

CONFER: *Guide questions for discussion*

1. What does psychological reciprocity mean?

2. Why is it easy to react as we are treated?

3. Why do you think man is hesitant to do well to others?

4. Is love the only cure for all conflicts? Explain.

5. If we follow Luke 6:31, do you think there will be good interpersonal relations among groups of people?

Marvin Marcelino

The Rule of Psychological Reciprocity

Whatsoever ye wish that man may do to
you, do so to them… Luke 6:31 KJV

"I hate you!", shouted the boy on a hill overlooking the valley. A reply came back! "I hate you!" said a voice from the valley. Irritated, the boy shouted, "I don't like you!" "I don't like you," answered the voice from the valley. Challenged, the boy went home and told his father that someone over the hill wanted to fight him. The boy was able to convince his father to go with him. On the hill, the boy proudly shouted over the valley, "Hey, you come out, I hate you!" The same word echoed back. The boy said to his father, "You see dad that guy over the hill is cruel; let us fight him." The father, sensing the situation, quickly suggested that his son change his words. The boy tried, "Friend, I love you." and the voice replied, "Friend, I love you." The surprised boy said, "Dad, that boy down the valley became friendlier. For sure we will be good friends!"

Psychological reciprocity means the reaction of humans as they are treated. People normally behave as they are treated. When you treat people well, they are also good at you. If you treat them as enemies, then you will be an enemy to them. You trust them, and they will surely trust you.

Most often than not, we are like the boy on the hill, what we do mirrors back to us. The mirror only reflects what you show it. When a Christian reflects Jesus, then people will see Jesus in him.

The problem with the boy on the hill did not start from the "other person down the valley." The problem started from the boy himself. He was getting into a picture that was not true. He made himself his own enemy. He pictured that the voice over the valley was for real.

Self-image is a product of how we see ourselves. Our internal needs, goals, aspirations, beliefs, philosophies in life, and attitudes constitute one's self-image. Notice that each of us behave in a manner consistent with how we see ourselves. If one sees that nobody loves him, he will usually behave in a way that shows that he is unloved. Therefore, he becomes aloof, sour, rebellious, or refuses to love because that is how he pictures himself.

Thus, marks the tendencies in man to live up to the label whether given to him or selected by him. One person may bitterly think, "I'm stupid!" while another happily announces to himself, "I'm great!" At this point, it is noteworthy that we understand every person. How each person pictures oneself, but it is most crucial to understand one's own self-image.

When we do not understand our self-image and the self-image of another confused person and mix them together, the result is a classic formula of conflict. Big trouble indeed, starting with misunderstanding.

Conflicts are present between two people, tribes, kindred, tongues, churches, schools, workplaces, and homes. Different people with different personalities, temperaments, upbringing, beliefs, and levels of understanding are causes and factors of conflicts.

Conflicts seem inescapable, but that does not mean you cannot avoid it or resolve it. What kills love is not death, but our misunderstanding, our hate our prejudices. What are riches? What is power? What is beauty? They are at the end vanity after all. What is even better than death and power none but a loving heart.

Self is limitless, opposite to how we think it is. It has a capability beyond our self-image. It has the capability to love and do well. George Sand concludes, "There is only, one happiness in life, it is to love and be loved." Two thousand years ago, Jesus uttered this concept, "Whatsoever ye wish that men may do to you do ye also to them for this is the law and the prophet." (Matthew 7:12

Marvin Marcelino

WHAT TO WISH THAT OTHERS WOULD DO TO YOU

- Love your neighbor as you love yourself (Matt. 22:39).
- Think anything but good report (Philippians 4:8).
- Apply to life the fruits of the Spirits. (Galatians 5:22).
- Treat others how God treated you (1Thess. 3:12-13).
- What a man thinks so his act will be (Proverbs 23:7).
- Be holy (Colossian 3:12).
- Be merciful (Matthew 5:7).
- Be a peacemaker (Hebrews12:14).
- Be humble (Matthew 5:5).
- Be patient (1Thessalonians 5:14).
- Be kind (2Peter1:5-7).
- Be honest (1Peter 2:12).
- Be loving (John 13:34-36).
- Be joyful (Romans 15:13).
- Be fruitful (John 15:4,5).
- Be gentle (2Timothy 2:24).
- Be pure (Philippians 4:8).
- Be always ready to serve (Proverbs 25:21).

PRAYER

Dear Heavenly Father, I confess that I have not lived a life consistent with Your will. Teach me, Father, to overcome this weakness. Jesus Christ has shown me how to relate to other human beings. I beg the Holy Spirit to direct my mind to wish only good for others and they do the same to me. This I pray in the name of Jesus Christ, my Lord and Savior. Amen.

AFFIRMATION

I am to think only of good and of noble things of others, for this they will also do to me. This I will do because Jesus commanded me to and because I am an agent of love.

Loving relationship give our lives
the most fundamental meaning.
Leo Buscaglia

We must love another or die.
W. H. Andrews

Take away love and our earth is a tomb.
Robert Browning

Marvin Marcelino

The Basics of Interpersonal Relations

CONFRONT:

TRUE MASQUERADE

Write your true characteristics. (ex. Kind, liar, helpful, rude)

Most of the time

____

____

Sometimes

____

____

Rarely

____

____

Never will ever be.

____

____

CONFER: Guide questions for discussion

1. Do you really and honestly love your neighbor? (A neighbor can be your husband, wife, brother, sister, relative, friend, co-worker, etc.)

2. How do you love your neighbor? What makes it difficult for you to love your neighbor?

3. How does understanding oneself help us understand others?

4. Give one example of a 'mask' you wear. Give reasons why you need to wear this 'mask'.

5. How do you know when one wears a 'mask'? How could you help a person who is trying to remove his 'mask' but cannot?

6. How do you see yourself after reading "My Identity with Christ as God Sees Me"?

The Basics of
Interpersonal Relations

Love your neighbor as yourself. Matthew 22:39 KJV

One day at a mathematics class for adults, the teacher asked, "What is the square root of eight?" One student proudly stood up and said, "Sir, I know, it is eight multiplied by eight times by itself." "Are you sure?" asked the teacher. "Yes sir, "I'm dead sure." "Okay, how did you arrive to your answer? Can you show the class by solving it on the board?" The student turned red. Admittedly, he said, "Sorry, I just know it in theory, but I do not know how to solve it." The class burst into laughter.

Loving your neighbor is just like knowing math and not knowing how to process it. Likewise, many people can define what love is, but could hardly apply it to life. Interpersonal relationships function by means of behavior and attitude cues. These cues are the ways or means of interacting intelligently and appropriately with another person. Does that sound theoretical? Set the theories aside, rather focus on the application and the 'how to' of loving another.

Jesus simply told us to 'love your neighbor.' He is telling us to do the same as He did to us – to love others. That is simple, is it not? Now comes the hardest part - the application. What are some ways to love one another? Do you know any?

One anothering means one person having a good Christian relationship towards another person. Alvin H. Goeser defined, "Good human relations are a matter of forming habits of understanding people, of being tolerant of others, of being considerate, of being willing to help others live more fully, of helping them grow and enjoy and make the best of their lives." Filipinos have two concrete words for one anothering:

Marvin Marcelino

pakikitungo (getting along with others) and *pakikipagkapwa* (being humane with each other).

The basic rule of good human relations is to think and talk in terms of the interest of the other person. It means to get off from your own 'thinking' and 'mine-world' and focus more on to the other person. "Jesus treated us far better than we deserve and as He treated us, so we are to treat others."8

Be Spontaneous

The first step in understanding others is to know oneself. One must look extremely close at one's emotions and see how deeply one is in touch with them. As a guidance counselor, I had observed many people have a hard time recognizing how they feel. When I asked clients how they felt, they would provide reasons like, "because there is no rain" or "because such and such is so." In short, they cannot just understand what they feel and why they have such views of emotions.

It is easier to identify the feeling of a child like when my daughter Mayumi was three years old. One can even predict when she is happy, her whole-body laughs. In addition, when my son Joshua is sad or angry, one will recognize easily. With children, there is no gap between feelings and acting.

Children are spontaneous. This lack of spontaneity in expressing feelings is one problem among grown-ups. Grown-ups hide their true feelings; they can smile on the outside but harbor hatred inside. We adults whether we like it or not we send messages and people read these messages through one's verbal or non-verbal actions.

Be Real

As grown-ups, we have learned how to hide and be selective with our emotions. We adults have one thing in common – we conceal our true emotions.

Does everyone wear a mask? Does everyone try to mislead others by putting up a screen? Perhaps survival in life has taught one. One finds it easier to protect one's own image than face the shame.

Masking is a defense mechanism that we use in the daily interaction with other people. We use this to hide one's true selves. Everyone has a role in convincing us to set up a false front or a screen. Unpleasant experiences during the earlier part of one's life contribute to the development of the habit of wearing masks.

We spend much time perfecting the guise of an 'acceptable image'. We use this whenever we believe that we are no longer attractive to others, even if it is contrary to one's true selves and true feelings. We keep our true image and defend it rather than face reality. This behavior becomes stronger every day the mask we show favorable and profitable on one's part.

Thus, we distort reality so that the world takes its shape the way we want it to be. When we do not face reality, we risk our lives. Our connection with and relations to other people suffer because we are not true to ourselves and to others. See yourself in this poem.

PLEASE HEAR WHAT I'M NOT SAYING9
-Towne

Don't be fooled by me.
Don't be fooled by the face I wear.
For I wear a mask. I wear a thousand masks.
Mask that I'm afraid to take off and none of them are me.
Pretending is an art that's second nature with me,
But don't believe me. Please!
I dislike hiding, honestly!
I dislike the superficial game.
I'm playing the superficial phony game.
I'd really like to be genuine and spontaneous and me.
But I need your help, your hand to hold,
even though my mask would tell you otherwise.
It will not be easy for you,

Marvin Marcelino

Long felt inadequacies make my defenses strong.
The nearer you approach me,
The blinder I may strike back.
Despite what books say of me, I am irrational.
I fight against the very thing that I cry out for.
You wonder who I am?
You shouldn't
For I am every man,
And I am every woman,
Who wears a mask.
Don't be fooled by me,
At least not by the face I wear.

What truth do we need to accept? Marcus Aurelius effects that "the world is determined by our thoughts." The wise king wrote, "For as a man thinks in his heart, so is he" (Proverbs 23:7). One becomes what one he believes. Each one possesses a certain degree of the desires to love, the obsessions to create, the dreams to control, always in search of meaning in life, the wishes to be first, and the desire of satisfaction and fulfillment.

A friend shared this article with me from *Our Daily Bread*; the Philosopher says, "I am what I become." The Capitalist says, "I am what I own." The Scholar says, "I am what I know." The Existentialist says, "I am what I perceive and feel." The Moralist says, "I am what I do." The Radical says, "I am not what I reject." The Christian says, "By the grace of God, I am what I am" (1Corinthians 15:10).

Know Your Purpose in Life

Perception plays a constant role in one's interpersonal relations. The messages that we exchange with another may vary in value, like the popular children story of the six blind men who individually understand what an elephant is like.

They came out with six different interpretations.

If only Christians will stand for the truth and be firm in what the Bible is saying, they will make a significant difference. Have we asked ourselves why we exist, and why we live in this world? We are born for a specific purpose. God wanted His own creation after His likeness. God wants His created beings to collaborate with the objectives of His creation. God wants a created being who will return love to Him.

Each of us is God's magnificent creation. One can express love to another the same way God has loved each one (Ephesians 5:25, 31). God has intended each one as the most important of all His creations. God has been active in recreating man in the image of His Son (Romans 8:29). When one has knowledge of oneself through Christ, then one will notice that each person is no ordinary person, but more than a conqueror through Him who loved each one. (Romans 8:37-39). James Baldwin is right: "Love takes off masks that we fear we cannot live without and now we cannot live within." One must know one's identity in Christ, one's true self and not by the mask one wears.

How long will you wear and show that mask?

Marvin Marcelino

MY IDENTITY IN CHRIST- WHO I AM AS GOD SEES ME
(What God has given me and accomplished for me through Christ)

I am *a child of God*. Rom. 8:16.

I am *a child of light* and not of darkness. 1Thess. 5:5

I am delivered from the power of darkness. Col. 1:13

I am born of the incorruptible seed of God's word. 1Pet. 1:23

I am *born of God* and evil cannot touch me. 1Jn. 5:18

I am *blest with all the spiritual blessings*. Eph. 1:3

I am *an heir of God* since I am His child. Gal. 4:6,7

I am *a joint-heir with Christ* with His inheritance. Rom 8:17

I am *a passerby of this world*. Jn. 17:16

I am a member of the chosen generation. 1Pet. 2:9,10

I am *Christ's friend*. Jn.15: 5

I am *an ambassador of Jesus Christ*. 2Cor. 5:20

I am *God's minister*. 1Pet. 2:9

I am a servant of Righteousness. Rom. 6:18

I am *a new creation*. 2Cor. 5:17

I am the salt of this earth. Matt. 5: 13

I am *the light of the world*. Matt. 5:14

I am *God's handiwork, His masterpiece* to His will. Eph. 2:10

I am *indwelt by the Holy Spirit*. 1Cor 3:16

I am never left nor forsaken by God. Isa. 41:10

I am dead to sin and alive in Christ. Rom. 6:6,11

I am *the enemy of the devil*. 1Pet. 5:8

I am *strong in Christ* 1Jn. 2:4

I am *more than a conqueror*. Rom. 8:37

I have been *redeemed from the curse of the law*. Gal. 3:13

I have been delivered from the power of darkness. Col. 1:13

I have the authority to cast out evil spirits. Matt. 10:1

I have *all power over all the power of the enemy*. Luk. 10:19

I have been *granted all that pertains to life and godliness*. 2Pet 1:3

I have the *immeasurable power of God with me*. Eph. 1:9

I can do *all things through Christ* that strengthen me. Phil. 4:13

I am *created to be the temple of God*, His dwelling place. 1Cor. 6:16

HOW TO IMPROVE YOUR RELATIONSHIP WITH ONE ANOTHER

- ❑ Treat others as God has treated you (1Thessalonians 3:12,13).
- ❑ Love your neighbor as you love yourself (Matthew 22:39).
- ❑ Think nothing but good report (Philippians 4:8).
- ❑ Follow the commandments of God (Exodus 20:2-17).
- ❑ Agree together (Amos 3:3).
- ❑ Live the fruits of the Spirits (Galatians 5:22).
- ❑ Be holy (Colossian 3:12).
- ❑ Be spontaneous.
- ❑ Be real.
- ❑ Know your purpose in life.
- ❑ Live out your identity in Christ

PRAYER

Dear Heavenly Father, I confess that my interpersonal relationship with __________ is not in accordance with Your will. Teach me, Father to overcome this weakness. Jesus Christ has shown me how to relate to other human beings. Though Jesus was God, He humbled Himself. I beg the Holy Spirit to humble my heart to have a better relationship with others. This I pray in the name of Jesus, my Lord and Savior. Amen.

AFFIRMATION

I am to be spontaneous. I am to be real to myself and to be what God has made me through Christ Jesus. I am to love others as God has loved me.

Marvin Marcelino

The moment we indulge in our affection
the earth is metamorphosed.
RALPH WALDO EMERSON

Progress is impossible without change,
those who cannot change their minds
cannot change anything.
GEORGE BERNARD SHAW

180 Degree Metamorphosis

PARADIGM SHIFT
List some of the unloving thoughts, characteristics, or habits that you want to change.

Can be easily changed.   Can hardly be changed.

______________________   ______________________

______________________   ______________________

Impossible to change.   Would take a miracle to change.

______________________   ______________________

______________________   ______________________

CONFER: Guide questions for discussion

1. What qualities must a changed person possess?

2. What motivating factors would one need to change his view toward another?

3. What would hinder one from changing his attitude toward another?

180 Degree Metamorphosis

*Do not be conformed to this world but be transformed
by the renewing of your mind... Romans 12:2 KJV*

I was a rebel when I was young," said an old man, "and all my prayer to God was Lord, give me the power to change the world." As he approached middle age and realized that half his life had gone without changing a single soul, he changed his prayer to, "Lord, give me the strength to change my family and friends, and I am satisfied."

Now that, he was over old man and his days were numbered, he began to see how foolish he had been, and his appeal became, "Lord give me the grace to change myself. If I have had this right from the start, I should not have wasted my life." 10

Whether one likes it or not, changes in the way we relate has been actively affecting others and change is likely to anyone. One may ask what the demand for this change is. Ever wondered why one sees and even believed or engage in there is at times a taste of something wrong? Specifically, if, it does not match one's intellectual standards, one usually rejects it and does only those according to one's own mental framework, as long as one is happy.

One's mental framework is composed of the belief system, intelligence, understanding, values, academic background, expertise, attitude, philosophies, emotional maturity, and experiences in life. When experience does not provide one's mental framework as one may require it to happen or as one wants it done, this person will terribly feel bad. When one claims, and it fails, one can hardly accept whatever transpired, then the conflict starts. The mentality that the world must fit one's thinking must change.

Metamorphosis is a process of change in appearance that starts and comes from within. Remember when Jesus said, "Love your neighbor as yourself," and imagine the people who have conflicts. The human reaction would be "God must be crazy!" Do we notice that what seems the right way to us is opposite of what God wants? God said, "Your thoughts are not my thoughts, and your ways are not my ways." (Isaiah 55:8) Since we are God's children then, we will only do what is God's will.

Paradigm Change

Here is an absolute one-hundred-eighty-degree turn around. It is the opposite of one's thoughts and feelings. This is a proposal where we put to end one's wrong thinking. Stop one's biases and our prejudices. Apostle Paul urges us about "renewing our mind, transforming it, or replacing it if it need be" (Romans 12:1).

"When love for God is supreme in our hearts, we will not think of glorifying self. The Gospel of the kingdom is designed to take men's thoughts away from self and direct them upward toward God and outward toward his fellow men."11

We see change needs not arise from other people. It must begin with us. Change must commence within one's minds, one's attitude, and one's very hearts! This is where change most starts. Is it possible for us to change?

Yes! It is. Remember the story of the son of a wealthy man, who came back and admitted how wrong he was? He confessed that he sinned against heaven and was no longer worthy to be called a son. The moment one changes, simultaneously a grandiose celebration will follow. (Luke 15:21) Friend, what a celebration there would be in heaven when we choose to change.

Prophet Hosea preached, "The way of the Lord is right,

wise is he who can discern. The righteous will walk with them, but the rebellious will stumble in them" (Hosea 14:9). "Therefore, let us not allow this sin to remain in this body" (Romans 6:12). "To this you are called because Christ suffered for you leaving you an example that you should follow His steps" (1Peter 2:21). Paul left us this challenge, "Whatever you do, work at it with all your heart, as working for the Lord, and not for men since you know you will receive inheritance from the Lord as reward. It is, therefore, the Lord Christ you are serving" (Colossians 3:23, 24).

"The moment you have in your heart," J Krishnamurti wrote, "this extraordinary thing called love. Feel the depth, the delight, the existence of it, and you will discover that for you the world is transformed." Make this your legacy in life, as Henry Drummond said, "You will find as you look back upon your life, the moments when you truly lived are the moments when you have done things in the spirit of Love."

Have you started renewing your heart?

WHAT TO DO TO CHANGE
HOW WE LOOK AT ONE ANOTHER

- ❏ Recognized that we are all victims of sin and "all have fallen short of the glory of God" (Romans 3:23).
- ❏ Remember, "Happy are the peacemakers" (Matthew 5:9).
- ❏ Respect others, for we "all are fearfully and wonderfully made by God" (Psalms 139:14).
- ❏ Recall, that we are God's workmanship (Ephesians 2:10).
- ❏ Always acknowledge that God is not finished with you and the other person.
- ❏ Always recollect the fruits of the Spirit, which are love, joy, peace, longsuffering, gentleness, faith, meekness, self-control (Galatians 5:22,23).
- ❏ Reflect that the ways of the Lord are right. (Hosea 14:9) If you are of the Lord then you will only do what is righteous.
- ❏ Unlearn the bad habits you have (Isaiah 55:7).
- ❏ Return to God (Malachi 3:7).
- ❏ Examine yourself (2Corinthians 13:5).

PRAYER

Dear Heavenly Father, I admit that I have this negative attitude towards __________, and I have a hard time seeing that person in a positive manner. Teach me, Father, to look at _____________ as Jesus sees that person. I beg the Holy Spirit to direct my heart to be totally changed. This I pray in the name of Jesus, my Lord and Savior. Amen.

AFFIRMATION

I am changed by the grace of God. God's ways are my ways. God's thoughts are my thoughts. I do what is right and I no longer conform to the ways of the world.

Marvin Marcelino

The love of mother and child is beautiful;
but there is higher love than that –
the love of one another.
CHARLOTTE PERKINS GILMAN

Loyalty in relationship is based upon trust
and respect. It can only be offered never demanded
LEO BUSCAGLIA

Be Devoted To One Another

TRUE TROTH List down all your activities during the last 24 hours with the time spent on each.

Activities   Time Spent

____________________   ________

____________________   ________

____________________   ________

____________________   ________

                                                        Total

Make a pie graph.

1. How much of your 24 hours is given to other people? How much time is given to yourself?

2. What reasons would hinder you from rendering devotion to your neighbor? (Your neighbor can be your husband, wife, brother, sister, relative, friend, co-worker, etc)

3. Why should Christian's be devoted to one another?

4. Describe a person loyal to another person.

5. How would you deal with a Christian not devoted to one another?

Marvin Marcelino

Be Devoted To One Another

*Be devoted to one another
in brotherly love... Romans 12:10 NIV*

Don't drive me to leave you or turn my back on you. Where you will go, I will go, where you will stay, I will stay. Your people will be my people and your God my God. Even if, the Lord will deal with me severely, only death can separate you and me." (Ruth 1:16-17)

Ruth's love story with Naomi is not another Hollywood fiction. The story is real. It is a story of two women with different religions, cultures, and ages. Both struggle against loneliness, suffering, alienation, and survival; a vivid picture of what devotion is. Filipinos could say the story in two strong words – *Walang iwanan* (none abandons another).

"Many a man claims to have unfailing love, but a faithful man who could find?" (Proverbs 20:6) To be devoted is to be loyal, faithful, dedicated, consecrated and dependable. Devotion is loyalty to the other person. It is a result of wanting to be on the side of the other person. When you are no longer in their presence, you feel yourself slowly melting. Devotion knows no limit, whatever the situation may be.

Devotion also means sacrifice, the unselfish giving of oneself, the placing aside of a very valuable thing in life for the sake of the other person. It is the giving of one part (ideally the whole if you must) of oneself, one's time, even one's life for the other person. Devotion is not time bounded.

The ingredients of devotion are time, effort, energy, sacrifice and a lot of caring and concern. At times when we are checked of our devotion, all sorts of alibis fly out of nowhere. The usual excuses are, "I am too busy," "I was out of town," "I don't have much time," "I forgot," and the like.

Devotion is one of the many ingredients of love. How can one say that he loves the person when he does not have a self, a time, or even a life to share? Jesus has shown us what devotion is. He willingly gave up heaven and came down from the throne of His glory. He left His glorious power, and He risked His honor of being a God to the point of sacrificing His life on the cross at Calvary just for the love of you.

We can love like Jesus did. Ellen White, a noted writer wrote, "Let your heart be drawn out of love for the people of God. Hearts filled with love of Christ can never get far apart. Religion is love and is of God. You have not the love that dwells in the bosoms of Christ. ...It can only flourish in the heart where Christ reigns. This love cannot live, and flourish without action, and it cannot act without the increasing fervency and extending and diffusing its nature to others."12

Devotion is commitment. How committed must we be to each neighbor? Are we only loyal to one neighbor because he can provide us our needs and wants? What if one can no longer provide the need can we still be devoted? No one can win commitment by force neither can buy it. One cannot even demand it. Devotion is offered and earned as trust and loyalty are earned.

Let us learn from the sun. The sun's power and energy depend so much on the mystery of God's immense power. The sun was placed there at the beginning of creation. Yet the faithful sun continues burning, glowing brighter than ever. The sun devotedly gives all he has. Despite clouds and storms, he is always ready to shine. Have you ever had a day when the sun demanded something in return? It is only God, the Creator, who supplies the sun's needs. The sun comes and goes. Every sunrise, he is always there, going down for the sunset. As reliable as ever, he is devoted to us.

Have you been devoted to one another?

Marvin Marcelino

COMMIT:

HOW TO BE DEVOTED
TO ONE ANOTHER

- ❑ Express devotion by heart not by mouth (Ezekiel 33:31,32).
- ❑ Be sincere with your devotion (2Kings 20:3).
- ❑ Be there always (Job 6:14).
- ❑ Be there even unto death (1Samuel 31:5).
- ❑ Do it by heart like serving the Lord (Colossians 3:23).
- ❑ Agree together how much devotion is expected from each other.
- ❑ Do not lose communication. Text it, fax it, page it, write it, do anything as long as there is continuous communication.
- ❑ Ask God to help you be devoted like Ruth was to Naomi.
- ❑ Set time for a certain person.

PRAYER

Dear Heavenly Father, forgive me for not being devoted to __________. To whom I could hardly fulfill my responsibilities. Teach me, Father, to be devoted like Jesus Christ who has been there for me even unto death. May the Holy Spirit help me give my total devotion to ________________. This I pray in the name of Jesus, my Lord and Savior. Amen.

AFFIRMATION

I am loyal. I will devote much of my time and resources to my neighbors and I am committed to do the same as Christ Jesus has done for me.

We may give advice, but we cannot give conduct.
AUTHOR UNKNOWN

Advice is least heeded when most needed.
ENGLISH PROVERB

Advise One Another

CONFRONT:

TIP GIVER
List some of the names of people...

1. Who gave you advice when you were distressed.

_______________________   _______________________

_______________________   _______________________

2. Whom you gave advice to when they were distressed?

_______________________   _______________________

_______________________   _______________________

3. Rate your counseling skills.
Low   1 2 3 4 5 6 7 8 9 10 Highest

CONFER: Guide questions for discussion

1. Have you experienced giving advice? Can you share how it went?

2. What qualities are you looking for in a person to whom you would go for advice?

3. Are we really obliged to give advice to distressed people?

4. How would you deal with a person who thinks he does not need advice?

5. How would you deal with a person who is fond of giving advice even if it is not necessary?

Advise One Another

*Let the word of Christ dwell in you richly, teach,
and admonish one another in all wisdom. Colossians 3:16 NIV*

"**M**EN, had you taken my advice, we would not have had this disaster," sighed Paul as the ship's crew tried to salvage what they could from the shipwreck. If only the centurion followed Paul's advice and not that of the pilot-owner of the Alexandrian ship, they could have been spared from damage and loss. Despite what happened, Paul did not blame them, but he continued giving advice and encouragement to the survivors. (Acts 27:1-22)

Have you run across the adage that says, "The worst men give the best advice"? On that ship, the centurion underestimated Paul's advice because he was nothing, but a prisoner bound for Rome. Who would ever consider a superior would appreciate advice from an inferior?

A troubled sailor, though skilled, whose boat is trapped during a stormy ocean does not need blaming or preaching or even reprimand. Anybody who can see that someone is in deep trouble has the responsibility to provide advice. That is what Paul did. He had been telling the centurion what would happen, but the centurion ignored a mere prisoner.

Man has his own difficulties; some are predictable, but most are not. People have different experiences; some have the least; some have the worst. Some people unconsciously commit mistakes, and some intentionally commit errors even at the expense of righteousness. Then they get in situations that would face either their dream or their downfall, for survival reasons. The moment we neglect giving advice, we step down from our sense of moral uprightness and spiritual obligation; the result is chaos.

Marvin Marcelino

Whenever we encounter people who are in the state of discouragement, fear, trouble, sadness, loneliness, hopelessness, rejection, resentment, and bitterness, loss, and sadness, it is everybody's solemn duty to give unsolicited advice and encouragement to push and uplift the troubled person. It is not to dictate to them their decision, but to show them choices that would help them out of their seemingly hopeless predicament.

A person in distress generally seeks refuge; some go directly to God, but most choose people –people unknowing also have trouble. You have heard distressed people share their problems to distressed people, a man to the barber at the street corner, a woman to the people at the parlor and card or palm readers.

Distressed people look for people who can provide advice. It does not matter if they are distressed, too, if they can be trusted. Therefore, they go to experienced people not necessarily professional, but caring, loyal, humble, optimistic, and God-fearing. Whoever they are, people in distress certainly do need advice.

If we ever enter the solemn duty of giving advice, let us be precise with our advice. There is wisdom in the Holy Writ that says, "The blind cannot lead another blind" (Matthew 15:14). Paul tells us not to be satisfied with just a phrase or two, but rather to let the words of Christ Jesus fill us that we be full of wisdom. Then, we can share something good to another person.

Galileo was right when he counseled, "You cannot teach people everything. You can only help them discover it within themselves." Ellen G. White, in her book *Education*, cited some principles of Jesus' method of teaching. They are: 1) Independent thinking. Allow the person to think for himself. 2) Reasoning; Allow the person to examine his own reasons. 3) Personal touch; It is best to consult one on one. 4) Self-test; Allow the person by his limitations to commit errors and grow from them.

Any truth, if properly taught, can make an impact in the

life of a person. Henry Brook Adams relates, "a teacher affects man's destiny, he never can tell where his influence stops." "Like Jesus the Master Teacher, His words bore with them a convincing power because they came from a heart pure and holy, full of love and sympathy, benevolence and truth."13

Have you been advising one another?

Marvin Marcelino

COMMIT:

HOW TO GIVE ADVICE
TO ONE ANOTHER

- ❑ First, be a friend (Proverbs 17:17).
- ❑ Be God-fearing.
- ❑ Know that without advice, plans go wrong (Proverbs 15:22).
- ❑ Let the word of Christ dwell in you. (Colossians3:16).
- ❑ Do not follow the advice of the wicked (Proverbs 12:5).
- ❑ Be trustworthy.
- ❑ Be caring.
- ❑ Be humble.
- ❑ Get wisdom, understanding, and insights (Proverbs 1:2-7).
- ❑ Note that experiences differ from each other; seek second and third options.
- ❑ Give options do not dictate.
- ❑ If you are having difficulty giving advice, learn from others.

PRAYER

Dear Heavenly Father, I disclose that the words of Christ do not richly dwell in me and my advice to _________ was terrible. Give me, Father, the wisdom I need to be like Jesus in giving advice. I plead the Holy Spirit to direct my lips that my advice be a blessing. This I pray in the name of Jesus, my Lord and Savior. Amen.

AFFIRMATION

The words of Christ Jesus richly dwell in me, and I have the responsibility to give godly advice to people who are in need.

Relationships fail not because they are wrong,
not that people don·t want to correct their problem.
They want their own way.
LEO BUSCAGLIA

It is vain to gather virtues without humility;
for the spirit of God delights to dwell
in the heart of the humble.
ERASMUS

Offer Humility to One Another

HUMBLE TUMBLE
List some of your habits or characteristics that are...

1. Humble in the sight of God   Not humble before God

___________________   ___________________
___________________   ___________________

2. At times I cannot be humble because...

___________________   ___________________
___________________   ___________________

CONFER: Guide questions for discussion

1. Do you consider humility a weak and shameful down grading characteristic of man?

2. What does it take to be humble?

3. What motivates a man to be humble?

4. Describe a humble person.

5. Is there an exemption to being humble? Can you think of something that you need to be proud or boastful of?
   Why or why not?

Offer Humility to One Another

*All of you clothe yourself with humility
to one another... 1Peter 5:5 RSV*

What is your servant, that you should notice a dead dog like me," said Mephibosheth as he bowed before King David. Can you cut yourself lower than a servant? How do you consider lowering oneself to a dog? (2Samuel 9:1-9)

Mephibosheth is no ordinary person. He is a royal figure, he had been with dignitaries, and he was a respected member of a once royal family. Now he only looked at himself as a dog.

Humility is being submissive or modest. It also means putting aside any shade of your power, abilities, strengths, talents, degrees, and analytical capabilities. Looking at self as lower than the other person. "What? I have spent half of my life just to jack up my status as a scholar, and you would let me lower my status for the sake of the narrow-minded morons! Look, I have crawled by sweat, tears, and blood just to be in the pedestal of glory and no person has the right to tell me to come down." How would one respond to that person?

Among the Greeks during the first century, humility in a sense is derogatory and the downgrading of the nature of a man. It was regarded as a sign of weakness and narrow mindedness. When we insist on what we think and feel is right, without giving a second thought, it is then that we commit the sin of Lucifer. That is the insisting attitude of not giving up one's pride.

Confucius noted, "Humility is the foundation of all virtues." Sir Thomas Moore expounds humility as a responsibility that is "to be humble to superior is a duty; to equal is a courtesy, to inferior is nobleness and to all is safety, it being a virtue that, for all its lowliness, and commanded those it stops to."

Oswald Sanders' book *Spiritual Leadership* tackled, "humility is the hallmark of a man whom God can use. It is the highest in God's scale of values; it is self-effacement, not self-advertisement." Humility is an elusive virtue. The disciples of Jesus struggled with it. Remember when they were arguing

Marvin Marcelino

about who among them is the greatest.

Pride is the worst enemy of humility and the first friend and president of hell. It is like a disease of the mind that breaks and ruins all godly actions or a worm in your treasury that eats and ruins your health. It is disparaging virtues by detraction and your own by self-destruction. It is the friend of flattery, the mother of envy, the nurse of fury, the sins of devils, the evil of humanity; it hates superiors, scorns inferiors, and has no equal. In short, until you hate pride, Love is not with you.

William Law gave a clear picture about what humility can do, in his book *Serious Call*, he exhorted; "Let every day be a day of humility; condescend to all the weaknesses of and infirmities of your fellow-creatures. Cover their frailties, love their excellencies, encourage their virtues, relieve their wants, rejoice in their prosperity, be compassionate in their distress, receive their friendship, overlook their unkindness, forgive their malice, be a servant of servants, and condescend to do the lowliest office of the lowest mankind." Paul warns us that if we ever think ourselves of something when in fact, we are nothing; we are deceiving ourselves (Galatians 6:3).

"It is vain to gather a virtue without humility," wrote Erasmus, "for the spirit of God delights to dwell in the hearts of the humble." To be safe remember that all steps going to humility are going down. "When trying to help the poor, the despised, and the forsaken do not work for them mounted on the stilts of your dignity, and superiority for in this way, you will accomplish nothing."14

Here is a story of humility from nature. Two goats meet on a narrow path above a stream of water. They cannot turn back and cannot pass each other, for there is not an inch of space. Instinctively they know that if they knock each other both will fall in the water below, and they will drown. Nature has taught one goat to lie down so that the other goat can pass over its body as a result; each goat arrives at its destination safe and sound. Try it. It works!

HOW TO OFFER HUMILITY
TO ONE ANOTHER

- ❑ Lower yourself. (Your ego)
- ❑ Be ignorant. (Proverbs 30:2,3)
- ❑ Be nothing but dust. (Genesis 18:27)
- ❑ Be unworthy. (Genesis 32:11)
- ❑ Be nobody (Exodus 3:11).
- ❑ Have a discerning heart (1Kings 3:7).
- ❑ Be a childlike (not childish) (Jeremiah 1:6)
- ❑ Be careful, pride calls for destruction (Proverbs 16:18).
- ❑ God resists the proud (James 4:6).
- ❑ High looks and proud heart is sin (Proverbs 21:4).
- ❑ Be humble for the proud will be destroyed (Malachi 4:1).
- ❑ Serve the Lord with humility and tears (Acts 20:19).
- ❑ Be meek, for you will inherit the earth (Matthew 5:5).
- ❑ Remember, all boasting is evil (James 4:16b).
- ❑ Be humble and be great in heaven (Matthew 18:4).
- ❑ Receive God's grace by being humble (1Peter 5:5b).
- ❑ Count others as better (1Peter 5:6).
- ❑ Be humble before the mighty hand of God (Philippians 4:13).
- ❑ Do humility if you want honor (Proverbs 15:33).
- ❑ To love mercy is to walk humbly (Micah 6:8).
- ❑ If you are slapped on the right cheek, give the other too (Matthew 5:39).

PRAYER

Dear Heavenly Father, I confess that I have been boastful and proud towards __________. I have a hard time showing a humble character. Teach me Father the humility of Christ Jesus. I plead the Holy Spirit to guide my heart to be humble in all my ways, this I pray in the name of Jesus my Lord and Savior. Amen.

AFFIRMATION

I am humble, for God wants me to be. I am to always show humility whether in words and in deeds.

Marvin Marcelino

If you accept them, then their worth is great.
WILLIAM SHAKESPEARE

Prejudice is an attitude of aversion and hostility
toward certain people simply because of their
membership to a particular group.
ROBERT EGBERT

Accept One Another

TAKE IT TAKE IT!

1. List some of your habit or characteristics that are...

Acceptable   Not Acceptable

____________________   ____________________

2. Ask another person to write your habits and characteristics.

Acceptable to others   Not Acceptable to others

____________________   ____________________

3. If you accept another person, which characteristics would you prefer? Place a tick on the blank.

1. __Behavior/ Attitude
2. __Physical Appearance
3. __Family Background
4. __Race or Ethnic Origin
5. __Personality

6. __ Financial Capability
7. __ Health
8. __ Intelligence
9. __ Education
10. __ Religion

CONFER: Guide questions for discussion

1. Give reasons why one cannot easily accept another.

2. Can you easily accept another person as he is without consulting your standards or expectations?

3. How can we accept another without reservation or condemnation?

4. Have you experienced being rejected? How does it feel? How did you react?

5. In what ways can you teach others to accept one another? How would you let other people accept somebody you have learned to accept?

Marvin Marcelino

Accept One Another

*Accept one another then, as Christ accepted you
in order to bring praise to God. Romans 15:7NIV*

"Please accept Timothy if he passes by your house," pleaded Apostle Paul to the Church members at Corinth (1Corithians 16:11). Both are complete strangers; one is unsure, frail inadequate, delinquent, wavering, a young teenager with a timid disposition. The other aged, experienced, decisive, determined, strong, persevering, firm, courageous, persuasive, and professional.

How they met, is perhaps providential. Can you imagine how these two got along together? A complete contrast, it could have been a disaster. Just imagine the generation gap between the two, but by the grace of God both felt accepted by each other. Both were not intimidated by each other's strengths or discouraged with their weaknesses. Both worked compatibly in God's work, during their differences. How did they do it? They accepted each other just as they were.

The opposite of acceptance is to decline or refuse. It is far easier to decline than to accept. We always scan every person we meet and each pass through our x-ray machine of prejudices and biases. Then classify people as 'acceptable and 'refused.' There are things in life we do not easily get used to; these possibly can be the hardest tasks we face. First step before we can ever love a person is to accept the person as he is. Yes, I said accept, and acceptance perhaps is the hardest task among the steps in this book.

To accept means to receive, to take to oneself, to admit a stranger. Acceptance is like allowing a stranger to come into your home. "Acceptance," informs Charles H. Morris, "is an ability to relate to others on a receptive manner, with respect for their individual honor and dignity, which fosters their ability to enjoy, to mature, to be and to become because each person is unique, and he can act and react."

Has anyone ever heard a story of Jesus rejecting people? What about us, how many have we accepted and refused as a friend? That is what we usually do, isn't it? "Christ's sacrifice opened the way so that the most sinful, the most in need, the most oppressed and despised may find access to the Father."15 That is acceptance!

How do we reject? Simply by snubbing the person, as if one does not exist at all. We stab the person with words that even dogs could hardly eat, just to paralyze the individual's psychological and emotional stability because they are different from us.

Acceptance is hard to do especially for people who fall short of our expectations, intellectual capabilities, behavior, standards, interests, beliefs, and position in life. We only accept people who think, act, listen and do stuff like us. Even among the Christian company one will notice this *kanya-kanya* ("to each his own") attitude. It is not "the same feather that they flock together", but because there is an invisible barrier between people, such as doctrine, culture, color, social status, or intelligence prevents us from accepting other people outside our cliché.

Why does one cannot simply accept another? One may wear a smile and conceal a rejection. That who fear and avoid rejection wears a 'mask' to be accepted. Those who wear the same 'mask' as ours, we easily accept. Leo Buscaglia alludes "if we are afraid to disclose our imperfect selves, we cannot expect others to feel secure enough to do so and we continue to remain strangers." Is it true that suspicion at times kills acceptance?

Let me assure all that nobody out there has the right to refuse anybody because we are "all have fallen short of the glory of God" (Romans 3:23). In God's sight, we are neither rich nor poor, Jew or Gentile. We are all God's children, (1John 3:1) therefore; it is one's responsibility to accept one another.

The Triune Deity: God the Father, God the Son, and God the Holy Spirit accepted us without any prejudice, and any condemnation. As a child of God, be accepting in your words, facial expressions, body language, tone of voice and eye contact of which can easily communicate rejection or acceptance. Love is blind of color, race, creed, culture, and status and is always accepting.

Ayn Rand preached, "Indiscriminative love for one's fellow man is the highest virtue." "When you love someone," said Leo Tolstoy, "love the person just as he or she is and not as you would like them to be."

Have you accepted one another like God's acceptance?

HOW TO ACCEPT ONE ANOTHER

- ❑ Accept others as God's children (1John 5:2).
- ❑ Accept anybody for all are victims of sin (Romans 3:23).
- ❑ God looks at the heart (1Samuel 16:7).
- ❑ Convince yourself that the other person is as wonderful as you are.
- ❑ Suspicion can kill acceptance.
- ❑ Watch your verbal and non-verbal communications.
- ❑ Remove your prejudices; you do not even have the right.
- ❑ Receive people with an open heart.
- ❑ You must love at all times (Proverbs17:17).

PRAYER

Dear Heavenly Father, I disclose that I just cannot accept __________ for a reason that ______________. Teach me Father the attitude of Christ Jesus who accepted me just as I am: a sinner. I plead the Holy Spirit to move my heart to be accepting of other people without reservation and without condemnation. This I pray in the name of Jesus my Lord and Savior. Amen.

AFFIRMATION

I accept all people without prejudice and reservation, for God has accepted me just as I am.

But admonish them
we speak to them a word
to reach their very soul.
QURAN

Admonish your friend privately,
but praise him openly.
PUBLILUS SYRUS

Admonish One Another

MUTE WARNING
Answer by checking the box.

1. When I sense that something is unjust or sinful and I am in the position to give warning...
- ☐ I do not know what to say.
- ☐ I fear that I...
- ☐ I feel nervous.
- ☐ I do not want to confront or argue.
- ☐ I am not frank / honest.
- ☐ I think people might misunderstand me.
- ☐ I just ignore it.
- ☐ I need several people to support me before I act.
- ☐ I ask God for courage.

2. Give reasons for your response.

____

____

CONFER: Guide questions for discussion

1. Why do we need to admonish one another?

2. Is giving admonition the responsibility of only the adult and older people?

3. How should one person admonish without hurting another?

4. How will you deal with an erring "influential rich" brother?

5. Are there exceptions or limitations for one to give admonition?

Marvin Marcelino

Admonish One Another

Admonish one another. Colossians 3:16NIV

Admiral Sir," shouts the ship crew, "a possible collision is ahead of us!" While the crew peeps through the pitch-black night, he saw a blinking light directly before them. "Don't worry, everything is under control" replied the Admiral. "I've been with this ship for twenty-five years, I've gone through the worst battle at the Mediterranean," added the proud officer.

The admiral looking at the light directly to his ship's path he immediately commanded to send off a warning signal, "Turn your ship thirty degrees to your right." The light before them answered back, "Turn your ship thirty degrees to the left." The officer replied. "This is an Admiral; turn you ship thirty degrees to the right." The light sends another signal, "This is a second-class seaman, turn your ship thirty degrees to the left."

The Admiral became more furious and sent another message, "This is a battleship! Turn thirty degrees to the right." "Speed up and send off red alert," commanded the Admiral, "we are going to war." The lowly light replied, "Warning, turn your ship thirty degrees to the left, this is a lighthouse!"16

It is our duty to admonish one another. Admonish means to call the attention of another person about a specific fault, or to warn by telling the person, to correct what is wrong, to give mild rebuke, to warn if we obviously can predict the consequence of a specific action. It also meant to reprove, to lecture, to forewarn, to tip-off or to make aware.

The Bible is right when it says, "Better is the poor wise youth than an old king who no longer knows how to take warning." (Ecclesiastes 4:13) Immature and close-minded people are those that do not want to heed the admonition. These people tend to assume, and think that what they know is always right, and other people's thinking is wrong. They think their experiences are favorable in all situations. They cling to their expertise, diplomas and certificates that make them people who never commit mistakes.

Among many cultures, only adults or the elderly people have the right to give admonition. Younger people are bound heeding to admonition, which is the accepted norm for centuries. A younger person has no right to correct or point out a specific fault of an adult or older person. Again, many elderlies argue that younger people have less experience, and that their limited knowledge and experiences are inadequate to correct them.

Older generation usually base their admonition with their experiences in life and usually close their mind to new values, new ideas and truth. If older people have the right to counsel young ones, then older people should also receive admonition from the young people. This is not an issue of whoever is experienced or not. The issue in point is giving warning to those who are doing unrighteous deeds. If a situation calls for a young person to warn an old person who eventually may hurt himself then it is the young person's right to admonish.

Admonish him as a brother (2Thessalonians 3:15). The point cuts through ages, culture, and generations. The text is silent about any age limit, whether from the old to the young or young to old. It is silent about race and culture. It is simply saying that whether you are young or old you can admonish, therefore, anybody young or old must heed to admonitions.

Some people learn the easy way, and some people learn the hard way. Nevertheless, we are duty bound to give warning to everyone (1Thessalonians 5:14). Seneca, a philosopher has this good attitude, "I'm glad to be corrected, in order that I may teach."

We have such great men, who were not afraid to warn people whether they were young or old. Noah admonished for 120 years. Jeremiah gave warning before arrogant people (Jeremiah 42:19). Jonah also gave admonition before the wicked people of Nineveh and Paul among the Gentiles of Asia. These men made the difference in admonishing people. Let us not be passive to what is right, not that we must but because it is the right thing to do.

If ever one would admonish another or give warning. Do it in a constructive and loving manner. We need people of the third millennium, a new generation to stand for what is righteous, who can call unrighteousness by its rightful name, and can be firm to the truth until his last breath.

Have you admonished one another and heeded admonition?

HOW TO ADMONISH ONE ANOTHER

- ❏ Lead others to righteousness (Daniel 12:3).
- ❏ Admonish as God's minister (1Peter 2:9).
- ❏ Get wisdom from God (Proverbs 19:8).
- ❏ Warn as a brother or sister (2Thessalonians 3:15).
- ❏ Give the word of Christ (John 6:53-63).
- ❏ Share what has been granted to you (2Peter 1:3).
- ❏ Let your ear heed to admonition. (Proverbs 15:12)
- ❏ Remember that God choose you and ordained you (John 15:16).
- ❏ Remember that you are a royal priest (1Peter 2:9).
- ❏ Be firm.
- ❏ Be gentle and loving.
- ❏ Be constructive and creative.
- ❏ Tell the person the consequences of a particular wrong action.

PRAYER

Dear Heavenly Father, I confess that I cannot admonish __________ for a reason that _______________ and I have a hard time doing it. Help me Father to admonish in a loving and constructive manner. Teach me also to accept admonition from another whether they are old or young. I beg the Holy Spirit to guide my heart to stand to correct and get corrected too. This I pray in the name of Jesus, my Lord and Savior. Amen.

AFFIRMATION

I will always have an open mind and accepting attitude for I can accept admonition, be it from old or young people.

Marvin Marcelino

Authentic relating means each person
is genuinely concerned for each other.
LEO BUSCAGLIA

The greatest gift you can give to another
is the purity of your attention.
RICHARD MOSS

Activate One Another

CONFRONT:

PUFF BOOSTER
List some of the names of people...

1. Whom you empowered?   How did you do it?

_______________   _______________
_______________   _______________

2. Whom you discouraged or snuffed out? Why?

_______________   _______________
_______________   _______________

3. Do you know anyone who needs to be activated to love and to do good works?

_______________   _______________
_______________   _______________

CONFER: *Guide questions for discussion*

1.   What makes one easily reduce one's active attitude?
2.   What attitude should one have to activate another?

3.   How can you empower those who are weak spiritually?

4.   How were you activated when you were spiritually down?

5.   Do we all have to right to activate another?

6.   What do you think would happen if everyone activated each other spiritually?

Marvin Marcelino

Activate One Another

*And let us consider how to stir up one another
to love to good works. Hebrews 10:24 NIV*

Why do we need to pump air into the lantern father?" Asked six years old Pedro, as he watched his father fix the Coleman lamp. "We have to make the lamp shine," replied the father. "How does the air make the lamp shine bright?" Poked Pedro. "We need to pump oxygen into the lamp. It helps make the light brighter. Without the air, fire will die by itself," concluded the father.

Like the lantern, we need power. We need supernatural power that will energize us to love and make good works. Humans possess the power, but this power similar to any other energy forms are discharged and depletes.

All power has source of origin. Electric bulbs should always connect to the source of power in order for it to light and shine; once cut it is off from the connection it suddenly dies out. Another example is the ember, once you leave one ember out from the fire and away from the source of heat, the ember will slowly chill off then die. However, when placed back together they glow. Similarly, to activated means to empower again.

Is there a need to activate one another? "The councils of heaven are looking upon you who claim to have accepted Christ as your personal Savior to see you make known *and activate* the salvation of God to those who sit in darkness."17 (*Italics inserted*). To activate means to get one be involved again or to energized, to mobilize, to regenerate and to empower once more.

Empowerment has been a household name with varying usage. Examples are people empowerment, women empowerment, teacher empowerment and so forth. There is a different kind of empowerment, a truly special empowerment. It is the God-given potential to achieve the full measure of the stature of men and women in Christ Jesus. John the beloved is correct when he read, "I have chosen you and ordained you that ye should go forth and bring forth fruit, and your fruit should remain" (John 15:16). Those fruits are joy, peace love, long-suffering, gentleness, goodness faith, meekness, and temperance. (Galatians 5:22-23)

Our only source of power is from God. The power of God is penetrating and assimilating. It quickens the lifeless spiritual nature into an active state. An empowered soul has these characteristics: it exercises faith in God, it improves our health, it becomes sanctified, it ennobles, it submits to the molding of the Holy Spirit, and it receives manner in the likeness of the divine.

"Love is the power. Character and moral strength are involved in this principle and cannot be separated from it. The power of wealth tends to corrupt and destroy. The power of force is strong enough to hurt, but the excellence and value of pure love has efficiency to do good, and only good. Whatsoever is done of pure, be it even so little or contemptible in the sight of men is wholly, and fruitful; for God regards more with how much loved one works than the amount he does for love is of God."18

The Loving Way
Marvin Marcelino

The loving way is the wisest choice,
often shunned.
The loving way is the best path,
often forgotten.
The loving way is the honored conduct,
often ignored.
The loving way is purest habit,
often taken for granted.
The loving way is the noblest act,
all the time is the best.

Marvin Marcelino

Each of us has the responsibility to activate one another in faith, in hope, and charity. People feel or become cold with their relations at home or in the church or any other noble endeavor. Discouraged people slowly drift afar and can lose them from our care. We all must get them close to Christ, for He is the Vine ye are the branches. (John15: 5) Apart from Him, we are dead for He is the way the truth and the life. Remember the many wondrous things God has done for you. Use this God given powers in you to activate one another!

Have you activated one another to love?

HOW TO ACTIVATE ONE ANOTHER

- ❏ Be the light of this earth (Matthew 5:14).
- ❏ Do love and do good works (Luke 10:9)
- ❏ Remember that God chooses you and ordained you (John 15:16).
- ❏ Remember that you are a royal priest (1Peter 2:9).
- ❏ Remember you are a chosen generation (1Peter 2:9,10).
- ❏ Be more than a conqueror (Romans8:37).
- ❏ Pump up the power in you (Ephesians 1:9)
- ❏ Pray for one another (John 6:53-63).
- ❏ Invite one another to do missionary endeavors.
- ❏ Share the unpleasant experiences you have and tell how you got out of it.
- ❏ Read together the promises of God.
- ❏ Boost one another's moral.
- ❏ Always speak positively.
- ❏ Encourage one another (1Thessalonians 5:11).

PRAYER

Dear Heavenly Father, I admit that I neglected my responsibility of empowering _________ to love and do good works. Teach me Father what to do and give me the courage for the glory of your name. I beg the Holy Spirit to assist me in empowering weak souls. This I pray in the name of Jesus, my Lord and Savior. Amen.

AFFIRMATION

I am active and I will do my best to empower other weak persons.

Tell a man he is brave and
you help him become so.
THOMAS CARLYLE

Most people only need a push
to bring out the best in them.
MARVIN MARCELINO

Encourage One Another

CHEERY HOPE

List some of the names of people...

1. Who encouraged me?   Whom have I encouraged?

____________________   ____________________

____________________   ____________________

2. Who discouraged me?   Whom have I discouraged?

____________________   ____________________

____________________   ____________________

3. Who needs most my encouragements?

____________________   ____________________

CONFER: Guide questions for discussion

1. How do you know if a person is depressed or discouraged? List some characteristics of a depressed person.

2. What act of encouragement can you do? Give an example.

3. Have you experienced encouraging someone and it turned out to a wonderful change for that person? Share your story.

4. Have you experienced a hopeless and discouraging predicament? Who were the people by your side and what did they do?

5. How will you encourage a person who...
   a. has resigned from faith and belief in God?
   b. is desperate about life's crisis/
   c. is feeling lonely?
   d. is sick and dying?

Marvin Marcelino

Encourage One Another

Therefore encourage one another. 1Thessalonians 5:11RSV

No, don't do it! You will only make things worse." As the stranger led her to the light, he recognized the famous actor. Then he exclaimed, "I could never have thought you would be driven to this. My wife and I never missed your plays. They helped brighten our lives." He agreed that he would never mention the episode to anyone. Her parting words to him were, "I have long thought that in giving everything to my audience, I receive nothing in return. But tonight, you have shown me differently, you have saved me from myself."

Eva Lavaliere was a famous actor who, on that night, was so depressed and mixed up that she thought of taking her life by jumping off a bridge into the Seine River. After that matter, she left the stage and the world, and died a saint... all she needed was encouragement! "19

All of us need a lot of encouragement, especially in these last chaotic days of earth's history. We need much encouragement from one another. Encouragement means one's support to console and to comfort. Encouragement is a person who may physically or virtually present with one to uplift and support.

Encouragement comes in varied forms. It may be a smile, a nod, a tap on the shoulder, a note, or just being there to provide comfort and reassurance. Jesus knew how it felt to be left out and discouraged. Christ knows what we certainly need in time of crisis. Many a time we feel emptiness, uncertainty, depression, lowliness, despair, and hopelessness. Jesus had been there too, and that is why before He left for heaven, He promise to send us the Comforter, who is the Holy Spirit, the one called to be at our side. That He did!

In times of despair, hopelessness, sickness and even death,

there are three ways by which we can be an encourager. To be effective encouragers, we need to understand that: 1) People are most encouraged by a person who has endured and surpassed a crisis greater than their own. 2) People are best encouraged by somebody who are there in times of need. 3) People are best encouraged by someone who is remarkably close to God.

In our society where most wear masks, some people may appear to be all right in the church or workplace or home, but beneath the "I'm fine, thank you." facade hides a heart so bowed down with guilt that it is ready to give up! "There are many in our world who are starving for love and sympathy which should be given to them."20

There are characters in the Bible who had endured severe trials, and it was their fellow believers who encouraged them not give up. They were Moses to Joshua (Deut. 1:38), Judas to Silas (Acts 15:32) Paul to Silas (Acts 16:40) to name a few. Without someone, to cheer somebody, who do you think would be our spiritual giants? Ellen White was right when she noted, "It is by constant exercise of faith and love that believer are made to shine as the light to the world."21

You, too, can make a difference. Emily Elizabeth Dickinson expressed a beautiful thought that says, "If I can stop one heart from aching, I shall not live in vain. If I can ease one being that's aching, I shall not live in vain."

Have you been encouraging one another?

Marvin Marcelino

COMMIT:

HOW TO ENCOURAGE ONE ANOTHER

- ❑ Be the salt of this earth (Matthew 5:13).
- ❑ Be more than a conqueror (Romans 8:37).
- ❑ Pump up the power in you (Ephesians 1:9).
- ❑ Pray for one another (John 6:53-63).
- ❑ Do this even to the least (Matthew 25:40).
- ❑ Be there! Be physically present.
- ❑ Meet the person where he is.
- ❑ Share your experience and tell how you came through it.
- ❑ Read together the promises of God.
- ❑ Boost one another's morale.
- ❑ Always talk with a positive attitude.
- ❑ Encourage one another daily (Hebrews 3:13).
- ❑ Encourage until Jesus comes (Hebrews 10:25).

PRAYER

Dear Heavenly Father, I confess that I failed to encourage __________ and tell him/her not to give up. Teach me, Father, to speak encouraging words and to be a channel of hope. I beg the Holy Spirit to direct my heart and mind in bringing hope and comfort to souls who are in despair. This I pray in the name of Jesus, my Lord and Savior. Amen.

AFFIRMATION

I live to encourage others. I am to stop hearts from breaking and ease others' lives from aching. I will not live in vain.

TEACHING: He who can does:
He who cannot teaches.
BERNARD SHAW

There is no teaching until another is brought
to the same principle you are in;
a transfusion takes place; he is you and is he;
RALPH WALDO EMERSON

Instruct One Another

JITTER COACH

Answer by checking the box and give reasons for your response.

Whenever I get an opportunity to instruct another…
- ☐ I feel nervous.
- ☐ I do not know what to say.
- ☐ I get cold hands.
- ☐ My tongue gets stuck.
- ☐ I fear to get into an argument.
- ☐ I get a mental block.
- ☐ I am not that competent.
- ☐ I think that is a teacher's job, not mine.
- ☐ I try.
- ☐ I thoroughly study my subject.
- ☐ I ask God for courage.

***CONFER**: Guide questions for discussion*

1. How do you like giving instructions to another?

2. Do you have difficulty in giving instructions?
    Rate yourself from 1(lowest) to 10 (highest).

3. What do you think is an effective way of giving instructions?

4. When does one not heed or listen to instructions?

5. How will you instruct a person who…
    a. resigned to listen to others?
    b. thinks he knows everything.
    c. is passive?
    d. is stubborn?

Instruct One Another

...you yourself are full of goodness complete in knowledge and competent to instruct one another. Romans 15:14 NIV

Read instructions said a product label. "Blah, blah, yeah, yeah. It is all the same," I said, as I pulled out the product from its package, and placed the product in the fridge, and the box into the garbage bin.

The next day, I wanted to cook the dish I bought from the grocery. Stunned, I forgot what ingredients should go with the dish and, worse, how to prepare the dish. "Oh! The label," I remembered. The box was kilometers away, riding the garbage truck, anyway I cooked the dish, and one may not want to taste it.

Why are instructions necessary? Instructions are to let us know the ·how to do· or the steps in doing a specific task. Often, we have a strong tendency to believe that we already know everything, and then later ask, "What were the instructions again?"

What happens when instructions were not heeded well? Conflict arises there is the blaming, then, reprimanding, arguments and disagreement, then ill-feeling, hate, bitterness, and so on. On every coin, there are always two sides, likewise with instructions. There are always two persons to blame when instruction fails: the person who gives the instructions and the person who receives the instructions.

To the instruction giver, a question please: One must give the other person the necessary details, so they thoroughly understand what to do. Never assume people ·understood your instructions instantly· and never place high expectation on the other person unless you have made a very clear ·what to do· or ·how to do. One cannot keep other people guessing everything one has in mind; neither expects another to see what one sees,

Marvin Marcelino

unless directed.

Take note about some parents who unexpectedly give the child a painful spanking because the child was not able to do what the parents wanted him to do. It is extremely confusing to the child. To avoid confusion and conflicts, instructions of all kinds, must be made clear and understood, this applies to everybody.

Giving instructions takes a lot of patience and guts. Patience is explaining the ·how to· in the simplest possible way. Repeating if it need be until the person gets the instruction right. An Arabian proverb talks about four different types of knowing, it says, "He who knows not and knows not that he knows not: he is a fool-shun him. He who knows not and knows he knows not: he is simple-teach him; He who knows and knows not he knows; he is asleep -wake him up; He who knows and knows he knows he is wise, follow him."

Guts are necessary it is where one evaluates how committed one is with his principles. Sometimes, we are reluctant to give instruction to those who need it. Either we are afraid, or we are just passive and have an ·I do not care· attitude. Guts are what we need, especially when instructing others about righteousness, about doing what is acceptable before God.

It is one·s duty, and responsibility to instruct one another (Romans 15:14). Being a mature Christian does not require a college diploma, a master·s degree, or even a doctorate to instruct another. Paul mentioned three requirements for a simple Christian to be able to teach: 1) One must be full of the virtues of goodness, which are honesty, righteousness, worthiness, generosity, humanness, goodwill, and charity. 2) One must have the wisdom to provide enlightenment, insight and understanding. Ask God help, that you are always ready to give. 3) Be filled with the word of God and the qualities of Jesus. Now you are ready to give instruction on righteousness and to love to one another.

Let us be competent to instruct one another in all readiness of mind (Acts 17:11), by searching the scriptures daily (John 5:39) and studying the law by hearing. (Ezra 7:10) Seeking the book of the Lord and not one of these shall fail. (Isaiah 34:10) Diligently teach them. (Deuteronomy 6:7) A famous Bible student counseled, "Build a wall of scriptures around you."22 Finally, when we do this, Lord Alfred Tennyson challenges us to remember, "Knowledge comes, but wisdom lingers" that we may be ready to instruct one another.

Have you been instructing one another?

Marvin Marcelino

COMMIT:

HOW TO INSTRUCT ONE ANOTHER

- ❑ Pray for patience.
- ❑ Set the learning mood!
- ❑ Give clear objectives.
- ❑ Illustrate the whole picture of expectations.
- ❑ Tell the reasons why it is to be done that way.
- ❑ Ask the other person to repeat the procedure to avoid confusion.
- ❑ Ask for suggestions for modifications if necessary.
- ❑ Give compliments for very good output.
- ❑ Allow room for errors.
- ❑ Do not give instructions with insult (It will never work!).
- ❑ Be creative in giving instructions.
- ❑ Whoever heeds instruction prospers (Proverbs 16:20).
- ❑ Listen to instruction and be wise (Proverbs 13:20).
- ❑ Study the scriptures to be competent before God (2Timothy 2:15).
- ❑ Remember that commandments are the discipline of life (Proverb 6:23).
- ❑ He who ignores instruction despises himself. (Proverbs 8:33)
- ❑ If one does not listen to instructions, his prayers are nothing. (Proverbs 28:9)
- ❑ Explore wisdom (Proverbs 22:12).
- ❑ Ask God for wisdom (James 1:5).
- ❑ Listen to wise sayings (Ecclesiastes 1:3).

PRAYER

Dear Heavenly Father, I admit that I lack the skill of giving instruction to another. Teach me, Father, how to instruct the way Jesus did. I beg the Holy Spirit to assist me so that I may properly instruct the Truth to others. This I pray in the name of Jesus, my Lord and Savior. Amen.

AFFIRMATION

I stand firm to the principles of the Bible, and I am to instruct the Truth to others without fear, that they may know God.

One may smile and smile and be a villain.
WILLIAM SHAKESPEARE

Let us always meet each other with a smile,
for the smile is the beginning of love.
MOTHER THERESA

Marvin Marcelino

Greet One Another

CONFRONT:

GREETER BEATER
Supply the names of people...

I always greet	I sometimes greet
___________________	___________________
___________________	___________________
I never greet	I wish to greet
___________________	___________________
___________________	___________________
I will never greet	I will die before I greet
___________________	___________________
___________________	___________________

CONFER: *Guide questions for discussion*

1. What reasons make it hard for one to greet another?

2. Tell the best way to break the "ice" when you greet another.

3. Why does one have the tendency to be very selective in greeting another?

4. How do you greet strangers? Share your style.

5. How could one's greeting contribute to another's experience of fellowship?

Greet One Another

Greet one another. 1 Peter 5:14 RSV

i, hello, how are you?" Said one ant to another ant, as they both carried a heavy load of grain larger than themselves. One time, I was studying the motivation behind their industry. I noticed that even during their busy day they still find time to meet and greet other ants all along the way. Their antennae and their eyes would meet for a split-second and off they go to the next. What is most notable is that they accomplish their task in unity and harmony*!*

Are we all born strangers? The first experience one has been the greeting of one's mother after birth. It was an exciting time when one came to earth and people looked and greeted you with smiles and happiness. We may be strangers to anyone, and it is not a grave sin to greet one another. At first, you will feel awkward, but eventually you will find that a smile usually reflects a smile.

To greet or salute means initiate a welcome. Greetings can take a form of a compliment, a bow, a nod, a touch, a tap on the shoulder, to connect, or to exchange a hand wave. Why do we need to greet each other? We greet each other because it is a natural human thing to do. Greeting one another is a form of communication. In other words, we are like telling somebody "I am glad and happy to meet you again."

What shall we do to greet? There are varieties of ways to greet. You can smile, nod, bow, you can shake the hand, tap the shoulder, and say, "Hi or Hello", or the common "How are you?" or just a simple sweet smile.

Greeting is the link that connects one and identifies one to another. It removes the strangeness of one, it gives one confidence, it even gives changes one's perception of another person. It breaks the ice, it removes the gap, it builds trust, and

Marvin Marcelino

it opens the gate to acceptance, friendship, and understanding.

Do we take 1Peter 5:14 literally?   An unsolicited kiss could bring you in court and could cost you a multi-million-dollar lawsuit. Let us consider the cultural background of the text. In Eastern nations, particular in the Arab world, kissing is one way of greeting especially to men. It is their culture. To some culture, seeing two men kissing or doing cheek to cheek or *beso-beso* is taboo and shameful, or even immoral.

To Filipinos, the concept of kissing is limited to the family circle up to third and fourth generations. Could we apply a holy kiss to our current society? Culture changes, in the past, kiss is given with genuine motives. However, in these modern times the distortion and corruption of the use of kiss. A kiss can turn to "*halik-ni-Hudas*" (Judas' kiss), which means worthless, suspecting, and questionable.

Desmond Morris noted, "The fear of touching was related to old, often unconscious sexual taboos- that made it extremely hard for us to indulge in any physical contact without implication of sexual involvement. A massive inhibition of our non-sexual body intimacies applied to relationships with our parents and offspring (beware, Oedipus!), our siblings (beware incest!), our close same-sex friends (beware, homosexuality), our close-opposite-sex friends (beware, adultery), and our many casual friends (beware promiscuity). All of these are understandable, but unnecessary."

Many times, I experience walking into a church, and I notice all eyes just staring at me. You may have experienced going the whole day, and nobody in the family greeted you. Let us learn to greet one another. We are no longer the kind of people who are apparently too shy to greet. Once you turn your back, one figuratively speaking hacks you.

A story told about a congregation who thought it was a sin to greet one another. So, they kept a formal face, which eventually made them more aloof, distant and, worst, suspicious of each other. You could feel how cold it was in their midst. Just then, one stranger a changed man, came and started to smile and greet everyone. Because of his contagious aura, he was able to rekindle friendliness and warmth among the church members.23

Let us greet one another as often as we can with a simple bow, a nod, a compliment, or a smile. Once you start, make it a habit. Have you been greeting one another?

HOW TO GREET ONE ANOTHER

- ❏ Make eye contact.
- ❏ Smile.
- ❏ Give a simple and sincere compliment.
- ❏ Give a tap on the shoulder.
- ❏ Give a nod.
- ❏ Greet everyone by name. (3 John1:4)
- ❏ Greet your superiors. (Hebrews 13:14)
- ❏ Greet them that love us in faith. (Titus 3:15)
- ❏ Speak good words to make the heart glad. (Proverbs 12:25)

PRAYER

Dear Heavenly Father, I admit I intentionally do not greet ___________ for the reason of ______________. Teach me, dear Father, not to be choosy in greeting brothers and sisters in Christ because Jesus was never choosy. I beg the Holy Spirit now to lead me in greeting my neighbors. This I pray in the name of Jesus, my Lord and Savior. Amen.

AFFIRMATION

I am to greet people without prejudice. I am to let them feel important by greeting them because they are children of God as I am.

Marvin Marcelino

92

Our inability to live in harmony
with others is responsible for our
greatest anxieties, feeling of isolation
and severe illness.
LEO BUSCAGLIA

Harmony is not found in self-contemplation,
it is perceived only when it is
reflected from another.
SAMUEL JOHNSON

Live in Harmony
With One Another

BLENDER BENDER

1. List some characteristics of united children of God.

_______________________   _______________________
_______________________   _______________________
_______________________   _______________________
_______________________   _______________________
_______________________   _______________________
_______________________   _______________________

2. Do you find such Christian characteristics among your group?
If YES, then praise everyone and encourage him or her to keep it up!
If NO, then start working it out, starting with you that others may follow.

CONFER: Guide questions for discussion

What are the reasons for disunity in the family, workplace, church, and government?

1. What can one contribute to have harmony with one another?

2. How can you make unity become reality?

3. What disadvantages are there to complete unity in all areas of life?

4. How would you deal with a person who does not cooperate for unity?

Marvin Marcelino

Live in Harmony
With One Another

Live in harmony with one another. Romans 12:16 RSV

Utopia is a dream world. If Utopia ever exists and its lots are for sale, it would be the hottest real estate on the market. Even if, it's worth millions of dollars, imagine living in a world where there is peace, harmony, no violence, no crimes, no laws, and no evil.

Would that be in the *Bubble City of the Deep Sea 2000* or a part of the *Enterprise* soaring in the galaxy of *Star Wars*? One just knows if it is an illusion. A wish to escape the chaotic world we now live.

One simple fact for the Utopian idea is that there is no harmony in our midst. Thanks to Sir Thomas More, we have at least something to look forward to or dream. Misunderstandings and conflict can cause disharmony – from the simple ones to the most difficult cases of crime.

It may seem impossible to live in harmony with one another as one may conclude. The Bible says it is possible if we try it. Read the context of Romans 12:16 and 17, there are certain principles Apostle Paul suggested for us to have harmony: 1) Do not be proud. This is the very sin that made Lucifer fall from his rank in the heavens. There is similarity in the root-cause one can trace in any conflict. 2) Be willing to associate with the lower classes of people. 3) Do not be conceited. That is self-importance, self-satisfaction, arrogance, complacency, immodesty, and pride (Romans 12:16) 4) Do not take revenge. 5) Do what is right to others, and 6) Live at peace with everybody.

One must know the cycle of disharmony it starts with self and ends with self. Take the word 'pride' and spell **P-R-I-D-E**. P and R stand for Personal Reputation - note the 'I' in the middle - and

D and E for Devil's Ensnare). Pride results from envy and jealousy. This is a simple formula for chaos and disunity.

Can we live in harmony with one another? YES! For Jesus said, "Blessed are the peacemakers" (Matthew 5:9). If only we all practice being peacemakers. The song written by Paul McCartney says, "Ebony and ivory live together in perfect harmony, side by side on my piano." We must accept that people have differences, like the keyboard. It has black and white keys – one can use all the black keys alone to make music and one can do the same with the white keys. However, to produce real musical harmony on the keyboard, one must use both black and white keys together. Christ's prayer at the garden of Gethsemane was, "we may be one as he and the Father are one" (John 17:11).

Ellen White preached, "Harmony and union among varied disposition is the strongest witness that can be born of. That God has sent His Son in the world to save the sinners. It is our privilege to bear this witness to do this; our wills must be molded in harmony with His character. Our wills must be surrendered to His will. Then we shall work together with a thought of collision little difference felt upon which led to action that destroy Christian fellowship, let us never allow the enemy thus to gain the advantage over us. Let us keep drawing near to God and one another. Brother is brought to brother by the golden love of Christ. The Spirit of God alone can bring about this oneness. He who sanctified Himself can sanctify His disciples. United with Him they will be united with one another in the most faith when we strive for this unity as God desires us to strive for it, it will come to us."24

In short if we are of God and with God who would be against us? Harmony is next to that. "Love alone is capable of uniting living beings," said Pierre Teilhard de Chardin, "in such a way as to complete and fulfill them, for it alone takes them and joins them by what is deepest in themselves." Djalal ad-Din Rumi adds, "Love is the energizing elixir of the universe the cause and effect of all harmonies." Are you with us working for unity and harmony?

Marvin Marcelino

COMMIT:

HOW TO LIVE IN HARMONY WITH ONE ANOTHER

- ❑ Surrender your will to God's will.
- ❑ Be a peacemaker (Matthew 5:9).
- ❑ Love the Law of God. (Psalm 119:165)
- ❑ Do not be proud and conceited (Romans 12:16).
- ❑ Do not be egoistic and envious (Romans 12:16).
- ❑ Do nothing from selfishness but count others better (Philippians 2:3).
- ❑ Honor one another (Romans 12:10).
- ❑ Say no to ungodliness (Titus2:12, 13).
- ❑ Set an example in love and purity (1Timothy 4:12).
- ❑ Unite with God to bring peace (1Corinthians 7:15).
- ❑ Strive to maintain unity and harmony with one another (Hebrews 12:14).
- ❑ Live peaceably with all men (Romans 12:18).
- ❑ Live in peace (2Corinthians 13:11).
- ❑ Have one spirit, one mind; strive together in faith (Philippians 1:27).
- ❑ Be in one accord (Philippians 2:2; 2Corinthians 13:11).
- ❑ Have one mind (Revelation 17:13; 1Peter 3:8).
- ❑ Do justly and love mercy, walk humbly before God (Micah 6:8).

PRAYER

Dear Heavenly Father, I admit that __________ and I do not live in harmony with my fellow men. My fault is that I am too ___________. Teach me, dear Father, the harmony You have with Jesus and the Holy Spirit. I beg the Holy Spirit now to lead me to live in harmony and peace with my fellow men. This I pray in the name of Christ Jesus, my Lord and Savior, Amen.

AFFIRMATION

I live to contribute to unity and harmony. As a child of God, I am a peacemaker, and I will do my best to make unity and peace a reality.

Do more than live: Love.
LEROY BROWNLOW

But drops of grief can ne·er repay,
the debts of love I owe;
Here Lord I give myself away,
·tis all that I can do.
ISAAC WATTS

Marvin Marcelino

Continue Having the Debt of Love For One Another

CONFRONT:

DEBIT CREDIT
Place a check on the box in each column.

1. If I am going to pay my debt of love, I need
   - ☐ The Knowledge
   - ☐ Confidence
   - ☐ A Seminar
   - ☐ Determination
   - ☐ A teacher

2. For me loving is...
   - ☐ Impossible
   - ☐ Beautiful
   - ☐ Hard, but worth trying
   - ☐ Okay but …
   - ☐ Too much of a commitment.

CONFER: Guide questions for discussion

1. Do we really owe love to one another? Why? Give your reasons.

2. How is one indebted to another?

3. Are we obliged to pay the "debt of love" to another?

4. In what ways can we 'pay' our 'debt of love' to one another?

5. Does knowing about the 'debt of love' do well for one another's relationship?

Continue Having the Debt of Love For One Another

Owe no man anything, but continue to have the debt of love for one another. Romans 13:8 KJV

Can I take my family to the high mountains of God?" A woman from the valley prayed, suddenly an angel appeared and said, "Before God is ready to take your home and family, set your house in order. There may be others who might want to stop by after you are gone."

The woman organized her house, and she became kind and forgiving. Then she said to the angels, "May I go now that my house is now in order?" "No," said the angel, "your garden is full of weeds; someone may want to watch a while in the garden while you are away." Therefore, woman weeded her garden and tended it for many years. She uprooted unhealthy habits in herself, like hates and grudges. Then she said, "Can I now lead my family to the mountains of God?" The angel shook his head; "There is a beggar outside your door, you cannot go unless you have fed the beggar and served her friend and neighbors."

All rejoiced because of her help. Then she thought she was ready. The angel asked her to do one more thing. "There is someone down the road who is also seeking God, but they have not heard about your faith and courage." Then the woman helped the weak and the discouraged where she found them.

Again, now she asked the angels, "May I now take my family to the heights of God?" The angels called in the family; the son healed from drugs, the husband bound her by the cord of love and service and the runaway daughter came home by mother's prayers, and even grateful neighbors came. The angel opened the window of the little house. Lo, her home was in the mountain of God!25

Marvin Marcelino

Who likes the word debt? Nobody likes to be indebted, not even the idea of it. Nonetheless, whether we like it or not, we are all under a certain amount of indebtedness. Each of us has our personal indebtedness. Indebted to the small dollar, we loaned or owed for whatever reason. We are indebted to people who made our life better. We are indebted to our loved ones for our neglected responsibilities and infidelities. We are indebted to our parents, our community church, and even up to God whom we are worshiping. We are indeed relationally indebted!

To be in debt is to be under obligation, to be bind. One must, or ought to return what is due to the other person because one owes another. Apostle Paul's advice in Romans 13:8 is very much relevant today. The first phrase applies to materialism. Owe no man anything, because being in debt is never part of God's stewardship program for man. He who owes another is a slave, and we cannot afford to be a slave to those who have.

While the second part of the phrase calls for our obligation, commitment, responsibility, and burden for one another. We owe everybody love. Moreover, we ought to return it back to whosoever it concerns, even to that stranger next door. Do we truly need to repay our debt of love? Yes, we need to, and we must. Jesus' command was "Love each other as I love you" (John15: 12). The implication is that God never asked us to pay for what He did for us. Instead of giving our expression of love to God, He desires that we will give it to others instead.

Elbert Hubbard wrote, "Love grows by giving. The love we give is the only love we keep. The only way to retain love is to give it away." Moreover, Thomas Huxley said, "Thoughtfulness for others, generosity, modesty and self-respect are the qualities which make a man and a woman a gentleman or a lady." Nevertheless, "We are not held back by the love we did not receive in the past, but by the love we're not extending in the present," said Marianne Williamson.

It is God's grandest joy is to see His children loving one

another. When one is indebted, he will learn sympathy and courage for his brother or neighbor. Love is the only debt any man owes another person and love is the only currency one can clear this indebtedness!

Have you been paying your 'debt of love' lately?

HOW TO CONTINUE HAVING A DEBT OF LOVE FOR ONE ANOTHER

- ❑ Love your neighbor as yourself (Leviticus 19:18).
- ❑ Do to others what you want others to do to you (Luke 6:31).
- ❑ Love, so that the love of the Father is in you (1John 4:8).
- ❑ Let brotherly love continue (Hebrews 13:1).
- ❑ Walk in love, as Christ loved us. (Ephesians 5:2)
- ❑ The love of Christ compels us (2Corinthians 5:14).
- ❑ Love your enemies (Matthew 5:44).
- ❑ Whatsoever is lovely... think about it (Philippians 4:8).
- ❑ Love all the time (Proverbs 17:17)
- ❑ Remember, we are debtors of good deeds (Romans 12:8).

PRAYER

Dear Heavenly Father, I admit that I never knew that I had a debt of love to _________________. Teach me Father to do this duty toward another regardless of his status, race, and color. I beg the Holy Spirit to guide me to those I am indebted of love that I may fulfill my duty in the name of Jesus Christ, my Lord, I pray. Amen.

AFFIRMATION

I accept that I have a debt of love to everybody and that I must 'pay' by being loving and caring and doing good for this is what God wants.

And ye shall succor men;
'Tis nobleness to serve;
serve them who cannot help themselves.
RALPH WALDO EMERSON

If we fully comprehend the brevity of life
our greatest desire would be to pleasure good
and to serve one another.
JAMES C DOBSON

Serve One Another

SERVER CURVER Fill in the blanks.

1. What hinders me from serving others? List your reasons.

2. What would motivate me to serve like Jesus?

3. Types of people I will serve.

4. People I will never serve.

5. Serving activities I can do.

CONFER: *Guide questions for discussion*

1. Do we really need to serve one another? Why?

2. What does serving really mean according to Mark 10:44-45?

3. How do you know that one is sincere in serving?

4. What do you think would happen to the Kingdom of God if we remove 'serving or service' from its foundation?

5. What would motivate one to serve like Jesus?

Marvin Marcelino

CONSIDER:

Serve One Another

But through love a be servant of one another.
Galatians 5:13 RSV

In the cold mountain region of North India, travelers are helped to keep warm in a special way. They take a small earthenware pot, put a burning coal into it and cover it up. They weave string around it and wrap it with cloth and carry it under their arm.

Three men were traveling that way toward a sacred shrine when they stopped for a rest. One traveler saw that some people were cold, so he took the fire out of his little vessel and lit a fire so they all could get warm. In that way, he saved them from freezing to death in the cold. When they wanted to walk on, it was already dark. Then the second took out the fire out of his pot, lit a torch with it, and helped all three of them to walk in safety.

The third member of the group laughed at them and said, "You are a bunch of fools; you have wasted your fire for the sake of others." Therefore, they said, "Show us your fire." When he opened his vessel, there was no fire but only ashes and embers. With these fires, one of the travelers had given warmth and another light, but the third man kept his fire for himself and found out that his fire had gone out and he had none at all.26

The word 'serve' is too often misrepresented as menial, downgrading and an undesirable virtue. Serving is an act that praises God. "I tell you the truth if anyone has done this to the least of my brothers, you have done this to me. For when I was hungry you gave me food, for when I was thirsty you gave me water to drink, for when I was a stranger you invited me, for when I had no clothes you clothed me, for when I was in prison you visited me." (Matthew 25:37-46)

Greatness lies, not in trying to be somebody but in trying to help somebody. Serving for Christ's sake is always significant.

Jesus gave us a vivid example: "And whosoever wants to be first among you must be a slave of all, for the Son of Man did not come to be served but to serve and gave His life as a ransom for many" (Mark 10:44-45).

As Ellen White writes, "Among the citizens of the heavenly kingdom, power, position, talent and education are to be devoted exclusively to serving others. He who is the greatest will serve others most unselfishly."27

In Ephesians 4:16, Paul compared a Christian to a ligament where every ligament is part of the whole body joined and held together. Every ligament has a responsibility to serve, not only he alone benefits but the whole body grows and builds itself up physically and in love. Indeed, everyone has a part to do. Serving therefore can come in different forms. You can choose any endeavor according to your spiritual gifts.

Serving is a noble act in the Kingdom of God, for it is with this virtue that the kingdom is built. Through unselfish love, God himself served man after the creation. His Son came to serve us. His disciples believed and served. Without this act of service where would we be?

Serving is a spiritual gift given to those who are humble enough to carry the task and motivated enough; never seek for something in return. All who say they are Christians but never serve are not sincere followers of Christ.

Serving comes in many forms. It may come in a smile, a greeting, a tap on the shoulder, a short visit, a prayer. Serving is most beautiful when done in the name of a sanctified care that empowers and encourages people.

One may not always notice that each of us is enjoying the fruits of the services of the faithful before us. Are we not then to give the best service for the benefit of those who will come after us?

Benjamin Franklin preached, "The most acceptable service of God is doing well to man." "God accepts the services of those only who are partakers of the divine nature. Without Christ, man can do nothing. Love for God and man alone places human beings on vantage ground with God. Obedience to the divine command enables us to become laborers together with God. Love is the fruit that is borne of the Christian tree. The fruit like the tree of life for the healing of the nations."[28]

Leo Buscaglia taught, "The degree of caring about others is a fact that can be measured by the amount of time, and energy we dedicate to physical availability." Lastly, Albert Pine said, "Whatever we have done for ourselves alone dies with us, whatever we have done for others remains immortal." Yes, the Chinese proverb certainly is true, "Love grows by service."

So, the question is having you been serving one another?

HOW TO SERVE ONE ANOTHER

- ❏ Love thy neighbor as thyself (Leviticus 19:18).
- ❏ Serve others with love.
- ❏ Be a servant serve like a slave (Mark 10:44).
- ❏ Remember you are to serve as not to be served (Mark 10:44).
- ❏ Whatever spiritual gift you have share by serving.
- ❏ Whatsoever is pure...think of this (Philippians 4:8).
- ❏ Remember that if you have done this to the least, you done this to the Lord. (Matthew 25:40)
- ❏ Serve your leaders without being noticed (Ephesians 6:6).
- ❏ Render service with goodwill as to the Lord not men (Ephesians 6:7).

PRAYER

Dear Heavenly Father, I confess that I failed to serve ________________. Thank you, Father, for Jesus, who showed me how to serve even unto the cross. I beg the Holy Spirit to direct my heart to whom I am supposed to serve. This I pray in the name of Jesus Christ, my Lord and Savior. Amen.

AFFIRMATION

I am to serve others without expecting anything in return, because to love is to serve, and to serve is the foundation of God's Kingdom.

Marvin Marcelino

Have you had a kindness shown?
Pass it on.
HENRY BURTON

It should not discourage us if
our kindness is unacknowledged;
it has its influence still.
AUTHOR UNKNOWN

Be Kind and Compassionate With One Another

PINKY PICKWICK

1. Kindness is ...____________________________

____

2. To be compassionate is to... ____________________________

____

3. I will only show kindness and compassion to...

____

____

4. I will be kind and compassionate even if...

____

____

CONFER: *Guide questions for discussion*

1. What are the characteristics of a kind and compassionate person?

2. What example can you give to describe kindness?

3. What example can you give to describe compassion?

4. Could we love one another without being kind or compassionate?

5. Should kindness and compassion be given in a very spectacular manner?

Marvin Marcelino

Be Kind and Compassionate With One Another

Be kind and compassionate with one another...
Ephesians 4:32 NIV

Stop!" urged Alexander the Great, as he stopped a soldier driving a heavy-laden mule to the royal tent. The soldier took a bag from its back and carried it on his shoulder seeing that the burden was so great for the mule, Alexander chanced to see the act, he was very much pleased that he called the soldier over and said, "The bag, which you have on your shoulder, is filled with gold. Take it as a gift from me. You deserve it."29

"Little deeds of kindness, little words of love, help make earth happy like the heaven above," said Julia F. Carey is right, and that is what we need. Paul is calling our attention to be kind and compassionate to one another. The word kindness and compassion mean tenderhearted, charitable, and generous. An adage says, "The smallest, good deed is better than the largest, good intention." An anonymous author wrote this, "you can scatter wealth at random, in large and a small amount, but it is the little acts of kindness from the heart that truly counts."

Kindness is never distant, for Christ's love compels us. (2Corinthians 5:14) First Corinthians Chapter 13 gives us a complete guide on how to be kind and compassionate. Kindness and compassion in thought word or deed means external control of self with others as a standard. It is altruism: always proper, always virtuous, always wins, it is right, it is spontaneous, it deepens the spiritual life, and all can practice it. It is never too late to practice them; it is grateful, appreciative, considerate, and special because you are tolerant, sympathetic, and courteous.

There are people whose life experiences were painful struggles. Their misery and unbelief made them unkind and uncompassionate. Kind words, looks of sympathy, expression of appreciation has to marry a struggling and lonely person as a cup of cold water to a thirsty soul. A word of sympathy, an act of kindness would lift burdens that rest heavily upon weary shoulders. Every word or deed of an unselfish person is an expression of Christ's love for lost humanity.30

Kindness means helping without being asked and foreseeing another's need. Doing what we know others like, drawing attention to another's good qualities, praising others, and defending them, showing concern for the handicapped, receiving favors graciously, rejoicing in another's success, encouraging, consoling, greeting others, smiling even when you disagree, forgiving another's temper tantrums, and sharing ideas. Kindness and compassion are the shortest, surest, safest way to heaven and holiness. Kindness has won more souls than either zeal or eloquence or learning and even Christians never converted anyone unless they were kind. The irony of it according to Dave Grant is, "generosity is a good deed that is done quietly, inconspicuously and is immediately forgotten." That is an absolute kindness done in secret (Matthew 6:3).

What can kindness and compassion do for others? They bring out the best in them, and that make them come out of their shell. F. W. Faber simply puts it this way, "It is always easy to be good when a person wants to be good. It encourages the receiver to go and do likewise. No kind act stops itself; it always wins in the end even when misinterpreted."

A kind individual is ever wanted everywhere, needed everywhere, and welcomed everywhere. "Love cannot exist long without expression. Let not the heart of one connected with you starve for the want of kindness and sympathy."31

Go, be kind and compassionate to one another, it will move heaven to earth! Lastly, remember what Dave Grant said, "Generosity is a good deed that is done quietly, inconspicuously and is immediately forgotten.

Have you been kind and compassionate to one another?

Marvin Marcelino

HOW TO BE KIND AND COMPASSIONATE WITH ONE ANOTHER

- ❏ Love your neighbor as yourself (Leviticus 19:18).
- ❏ Do not show off kindness (Matthew 6:3).
- ❏ Be motivated by love.
- ❏ Imitate the Father-Jesus relationship.
- ❏ Be available to do kindness.
- ❏ Be compelled by Christ's love (2Corinthians 5:14).
- ❏ Remember compassion is an active action word.
- ❏ Make a difference by being compassionate (Jude 22).
- ❏ Show mercy and compassion every man to his brother (Zechariah 7:9).
- ❏ Do well God is pleased (Hebrews 13:16).

PRAYER

Dear Heavenly Father, I concede that I am not that kind and compassionate to ________________. Teach me Father the kind of compassion and kindness Jesus has. I beg the Holy Spirit to cleanse my heart of selfishness, that I would be kind and compassionate. This I pray in the name of Jesus Christ, my Lord. Amen.

AFFIRMATION

I am a child of a kind and compassionate God, and I will render simple acts of kindness and compassion to everybody.

See people as good and beautiful even
when they are trying hard not
to appear so.
LEO BUSCAGLIA

He builds better than he knew,
the conscious stone to beauty grew.
RALPH WALDO EMERSON

Marvin Marcelino

Build Up One Another

PUFF UP BUILDERS
Place names of your friends or family members on the blank.

1. My relationship with ...

____________ is okay. I build him / her up. He / She builds me up.

____________ is not okay. I build him / her up. He / She does not build me up.

____________ is not okay. I do not build him / her up. He / She builds me up.

____________ is a wreck. I do not build him / her up. He / She does not build me up.

2. For me to build up others I need to...

____

____

1. What makes it hard for us to build up one another?

2. How do you deal with people tearing down others?

3. How do you feel when being torn down by another?

4. Could we say we love without building up one another?

5. How can we build up one another? Give 3 examples.

Build Up One Another

Build one another up... 1Thessalonians 5:11 RSV

Please continue doing good. You are no longer children of darkness, but you are now children of Light. Get up be ready! Wear your faith, love and hope. We are not losers; we are to receive our salvation through Christ Jesus. Okay, up on your feet," Paul firmly commanded the Thessalonians. Imagine Paul, a former commander-in-chief of a legion boosting the morale of his army recruits, who had been under fire and almost at the brink of losing the spiritual battle (2Thessalonians 1:3).

Apostle Paul knew what to give his beloved brethren at Thessalonica. A strong moral booster is all they needed and off they went again to face criticism and persecution. Paul simply built up the brethren.

Let us work in building people up, not tearing them down. How do we build one another up? Take the example of Jesus: he knew what Peter needs, to keep going in faith as Peter was unconsciously being overcome by evil (Luke 22:31). How Jesus built up the street woman sentenced to death that committed grave sin in the eyes of God and man. She was not condemned; instead, she was given another chance and was told to stop sinning (John 8:11). The socially castrated and rejected Samaritan woman, where mere looks at her is already a crime. Jesus came to boost her hope, faith, and morale, and she felt accepted (John 4:7-26). At the pool of Bethesda, a man embraced his traditional belief about miracles and stayed by the pool for thirty-eight long years. Jesus came build him up and change his life.

Is this not what Jesus is telling us, "Stand up, you don't have to stay this way. You are better than what you think you are, take up your bed and walk." Like Jesus, let us work in building people up not tearing them down. *Oikodomeite* is the Greek word for

Marvin Marcelino

'build up' which is in the active form meaning to build, to raise, to establish, to shape, to form. If we love each other; we will actively raise one's positive qualities, establish one's good reputation, and shape each in a right Christian attitude despite one's weaknesses and past. We always look at the person as a new creation in Christ Jesus.

Why is it easier to tear down another than to build him up? We tear down people by gossip, smear campaigns. Negative word about the person destroys any person's reputation.

Be careful to those who stand aloof, those who talk about other people, whose world will stop if they cannot say anything hurtful about another person. Satan used that same tactic in the Garden of Eden. With our state of being sinful and fallen short of the glory of God (Romans 3:23), the enemies of God are capitalizing on our being sinful. The enemies of God trample us by our inabilities, errors, and pasts, and by these, they judge us. Prejudging is one way of tearing down another (Romans 14:10). God forbids man to judge anybody; and no one was given the right to judge another.

Ever since the fall of man, God has been busy building up the fallen nature of man with boundless love to every one of us even though we are not worthy to receive it. He always gives us another chance. God had been showering of forgiveness, salvation, justification, righteousness, and holiness for us to be back in the original state of creation – a sinless being. In short, God has been building us up through His love, mercy, and grace since the fall of man.

How do we build one another? The article "*99 Ways to Say 'Very Good*'", has some esteem building notes namely; "That's it," "Nice Job," "Try again," "I'm proud of you," "You really worked hard," and the list continues. If someone is tempted to tell you about someone else's life and it is tearing down the person's reputation, shun and reprimand that person.

One may have his strengths while others are strong in their

weaknesses, but all of us have them both. Who is perfect anyway, yes, no human is perfect, the more reasons we need to build each other up. Love is always building up. It puts beauty on every person it touches. It gives hope to the discouraged. New strength rises to those that are weak. It helps the despairing to rise again. It makes life meaningful to everyone. Felix Adler explains, "Love is the expansion of two natures in such fashion that each includes the other, each is enriched by the other."

Have you been building up one another?

Marvin Marcelino

COMMIT:

HOW TO BUILD UP ONE ANOTHER

- ❏ Always build up your neighbor as yourself (1Thessalonians 5:11).
- ❏ Do build others through love.
- ❏ Imitate the Father-Jesus relationship (John 17).
- ❏ For Christ love compels us (2Corinthians 5:14).
- ❏ When you do build others, you will be rewarded (Proverbs 10:17).
- ❏ Show mercy and compassion every man to his brother (Zechariah 7:9).
- ❏ Do well God is pleased (Hebrews 13:16).
- ❏ Tell only of other people's positive characteristics.
- ❏ Pray for others that they may overcome their weaknesses.
- ❏ Let go of any prejudices, do not judge.
- ❏ Say no to talebearers and gossips.

PRAYER

Dear Heavenly Father, I confess that I tore down ________________'s reputation, of which I know you do not approve. Help me Father to overcome this weakness for Jesus died for others that they may be built up for your salvation. I beg the Holy Spirit to anoint my lips to speak only righteousness to build up another's reputation. This I pray in the name of Jesus Christ my Lord my Savior. Amen.

AFFIRMATION

I am only to build up others. For God has sacrificed His only begotten Son Jesus for others to be built up and the Kingdom of God to be established.

We develop communication systems to
permit man on earth to talk with man on the moon.
Yet mother often cannot talk with daughter, father
to son, black to white, labor with management,
democracy with communism
HADLEY READ

Loving relationship depends upon open,
honest beautiful communication.
LEO BUSCAGLIA

Speak To One Another

CONFRONT:

WALKIE TALKIE

1.   I will only speak to _______________________
because ____

2.   I will never speak to _______________________
because____

3.   I like talking about...______________________

4. Rate how you speak.   **Poor**   **Fair**   **Good**

Clear	1	2	3	4	5	6	7	8	9	10
Full of Wisdom	1	2	3	4	5	6	7	8	9	10
Precise	1	2	3	4	5	6	7	8	9	10
True	1	2	3	4	5	6	7	8	9	10
Face to face	1	2	3	4	5	6	7	8	9	10

CONFER: *Guide questions for discussion*

1.   What makes it so difficult for one to speak to another? Give some reasons why.

2.   Should a Christian be selective with whom he speaks to?

3.   Is it fair not to communicate with people with whom you have conflict?

4.   How can we avoid and guard our lips from speaking evil?

5.   How should one's communication be? Expound some biblical principles.

Speak To One Another

Speak to one another... Zechariah 8:16 NIV

To speak is to communicate. One should notice that very few people directly go to the person and talk straight from the heart. Some people need a push or pull to talk. Figuratively speaking, some people have their tongues run back and short, but when people turn his back, the tongue is doubly longer than normal. One can effectively communicate if there is the willingness to hear new ideas, or a desire to establish a relationship and to listen attentively.

Man is a created talking creature. Why do we have this fear of speaking or communicating with one another? There more audience type people who prefer to sit back in a corner of a gathering and watch, rather than express one's thoughts.

Take note of how cold it is in the bus or train as if we must maintain public silence. Those who dare to talk are considered manner less and are so courageous to break the unwritten laws of silence in public places. Does anybody know that some people are just waiting at someone to talk to them?

There are three communication killers: 1) the fear of sharing private matters or getting involved, 2) the fear of rejection by criticism or being ignored, 3) the fear to accept new insights and ideas.

Leo Buscaglia lectured, "Many find it threatening to communicate love. Unexpressed love is the greatest cause of sorrow and regrets. We, usually wait until people have died to express this value in our lives, to honor them publicly and to express our love for them."

Communicate! Share something with another. Do not be afraid. You have the right to express your thoughts, your feelings, to share what you know. The Wise king has written in Proverbs 25:11, "A word nicely spoken is like an apple in the silver setting."

Marvin Marcelino

Take note how and what we speak to and of other. The difficult part in communication is the silent communication. Silence when used wrongly at times is misleading and always the source of misunderstanding. It is always better speaking up face to face so that our understanding and joy may be full. Be cautious if you tend to talk a lot. Phillip Brooks said, "A man lives with rights and his right has more power in his silence than another by his words." Remember your Constitutional right to freedom of speech. Yes, you can speak, but it has its limits because one can abuse one's noble right to speak. Always place your speaking in the right place at the right time and the right tone.

Will Carleton has good advice, "be careful with fire" - careful with words ten times doubly. Also, take note of what you speak, as the adage says, "Idle minds speak about people, big mind speaks about facts, but great minds talk about ideas." As we speak let us ask ourselves these questions. 1) Is it right? 2) Is it fair with others? 3) Is it worth telling?

Unexpressed thoughts may sometimes not good for us, but once spoken respectfully, both benefits (2John12). Be willing to communicate (1Timothy 6:18). It is frankness to speak from the shoulder; it is intelligence to speak straight from the head. Speak words that suit the occasion, speak words that fit the facts, speak words that are quieting, not wild, speak words that are beneficial not harmful, speak words that are sympathetic not hateful, and most of all speak words of love and with love all the time.

Let us have a Talk Check: Watch the people whom you speak. Examine your emotions. If you are nervous, drink a glass of water. Practice how to be a good listener. Let one's speech always be with grace (Colossian 4:6). Let no corrupt communication come out of one's mouth (Ephesians 4:29). We must guard our mouth to preserve life (Proverbs 13:3). "The cheap talk, the words of flattery, the criticism, and talks to create a laugh are merchandise of Satan."32 Martin Luther urged us to be like his Savior, "when Jesus utters a word, he opens His mouth so wide that it embraces all heaven and earth even though the word be but a whisper of love."

Have you been speaking to one another?

HOW TO SPEAK TO ONE ANOTHER

❑ Remember there is a time to be silent and a time to speak (Ecclesiastes 3:7).

❑ Imitate the Father-Jesus communication (John 17).

❑ Speak slow and precise (James 1:19).

❑ Remember, "Pleasant words are like honeycomb (Proverbs 16:24).

❑ Let your speech be always with grace (Colossians 4:6).

❑ Let no corrupt communication come out of your mouth (Ephesians 4:29).

❑ Guard you mouth to preserve your life (Proverbs 13:3).

❑ Make your tongue, the tongue of the wise that brings healing (Proverbs 12:18).

❑ Lessen words that are foolish they commit more sin (Proverbs 10:19).

❑ Make your lips, the lips of the righteous can feed many (Proverbs 10:20).

❑ Soul rejoices when we speak the truth (Proverbs 23:16).

❑ Speak before God for up building (2Cor. 12:19).

❑ Speak face to face (2John 12).

❑ Be willing to communicate (1Timothy 6:18).

❑ Speak to one another those who fear the Lord (Mal 3:16).

PRAYER

Dear Heavenly Father, I confess that my communication with ______________ is __________________. Help me Father to speak words of love, like the words of Jesus that gives hope and life. I beg the Holy Spirit to cleanse my mouth, that my words may be acceptable before You. This I pray in the name of Jesus Christ, my Lord and Savior. Amen.

AFFIRMATION

I am a child of Love, for God is love and I am a vessel filled with love. I only speak of faith, hope, and love.

Marvin Marcelino

When you want to get even with another,
it is a sign and a conclusive proof;
you feel inferior to them.
A. E. WIGGAM

Jesus being a God, humbled himself
and became obedient to death
even on a cross.
APOSTLE PAUL

Submit To One Another

CONFRONT:

HUMBLEBEE
Complete the statement.

1. To me submitting to another person means...

____

2. List names of those you live or work with:

People I totally submit to: _______________________________

People I partially submit to: _______________________________

People I conditionally submit to: _______________________

People I will never submit to: _______________________________

CONFER: Guide questions for discussion

1. Why is it hard for one to submit to another? Give some reasons.

2. To submit is to compromise. Agree or disagree? Defend your answer.

3. To submit is a sign of weakness. Agree or disagree?

4. How can submission be seen as character strength?

5. What valid reason is there for you not submit to another?

Marvin Marcelino

Submit To One Another

Submit to one another... Ephesians 5:21 NIV

In 1989, while serving as executive director of the Master Guide Club at Adventist University of the Philippines, I had an assistant who took care of the one hundred fifty local and international new trainees for youth leadership. The training was a para-military class where discipline and obedience are necessary. During enlistment day, my assistant's opening salvo was, "Just remember that no matter how hard the task your officers want you to do, you always have the last word!" All the new trainees looked at him with surprise, and he said, "The word is Yes sir!" Ten months later, seventy-five submissive youth leaders survived the training.

The Greek word for submit is *hupotasso*, which means to be under obedience, to place oneself under inferior position, not in active upright position. It is not the argument of degrading oneself; it is a matter of sinking one' head regardless of one's position. It does not tell one to relinquish one's post of duty; it does tell one to listen.

To submit does not place one down, rather it uplifts one, it places one near God's favor because he is surrendering to God with all reverence.

An Italian proverb says, "Do you have fifty friends? It is not enough. Do you have one enemy? It is too much." Dr. Seabury, in his book *The Art of Selfishness*, says, "People fight for the sake of fighting." Never fight to inflate your ego. Never fight to exact your pride. Never fight to overcome one's adversary or to punish him. Fight without fighting. One wins by yielding."

Submission is the responsibility of a subordinate to a superior or a member to a leader. Submission is an attitude as to what position it calls for. Submission is an article of reconciliation. Submission is a way out of a forest fire of misunderstanding; it is where you cannot pass without changing one's attitude.

Submission is one road to Christianity. Submission is also reconciliation.   Reconciliation is the healing of a broken relationship. We need only to give way to warm embraces when words of accusation changed to words of forgiveness. God reconciled us to himself through Christ and gave us the ministry of reconciliation (2Corinthians 5:18). To reconcile is to remove animosity between parties and persons through submission. Paul is very much concerned about the horizontal reconciliation among Christians.

Ellen G. White in her book *Christ's Object Lessons* said, "No distinguishing on account of nationality, race or caste is recognized by God, he is the maker of all mankind. All men are one family by creation, and all are one through redemption. Christ came to destroy every wall of partition, to throw over all compartments of the Temple that every soul may have access to God." "In Christ there is neither Jew nor Greek, bound nor free are all brought nigh by His precious blood"33 (Galatians 3:28).

We are submitting out of reverence to God! Reconciliation is triangular - You to God, I to God and I to you. When that is complete, the ministry of reconciliation is complete, and submission to one another made perfect. Take Jesus as an example. "Consider him who endured from sinners such hostility, that you may not grow weary or fainthearted." (Hebrews 12:3) Remember Jesus Christ who, being God, did not make himself equal with God but took the role of a slave and was obedient and submissive even unto death on the cross (Philippians 2:1-8). Is that not submission?

Have you been submitting to one another?

Marvin Marcelino

COMMIT:

HOW TO SUBMIT TO ONE ANOTHER

- ❑ Submit yourself to God (James 4:7).
- ❑ Submit to your leaders (Hebrews 13:17).
- ❑ Be subject to one another out of reverence for God (Ephesians 5:21).
- ❑ Do not let the sun go down without reconciliation (Ephesians 4:26).
- ❑ You that are young be subject to …the elders (1Peter 5:5).
- ❑ Be subject to human institutions (1Peter 2:13).
- ❑ Be subject to your government (Romans 13).
- ❑ Be a peacemaker (Matthew 5:9).
- ❑ Be meek (Matthew 5:5).
- ❑ Be repairer of the breach (Isaiah 58:12).
- ❑ Use gentle words (Proverbs 15:1).

PRAYER

Dear Heavenly Father, I admit that I do not like to submit to _______________ because _______________________________. Teach me, Father, to be humble and submissive like Jesus. I beg the Holy Spirit to guard my heart from pride, for I am supposed to be submissive and humble. This I pray in the name of Jesus Christ, my Lord and Savior. Amen.

AFFIRMATION

I am humble and submissive to all even unto death for this is Christ's way. His death is proof of this.

Our greatest duty and our
main duty is to help others…
and if you can·t help
would you please not hurt them?
DALAI LAMA

Love…includes fellowship in suffering,
in joy, and in effort.
ALBERT SCHWEITZER

Marvin Marcelino

Bear One Another

CONFRONT:

BUTRESS BUTCHER
Place a check on the box.

1. To comment about how I bear another I would say…

[] I do not know how   [] I cannot give up my pride.
[] I can't do it   [] It's others turn
[] I think it stupid   [] I need a sample
[] I'm not a martyr   [] Pray for me
[] I need a seminar   [] It is something I need help with
[] I need direction   [] I just do not care about it.

2. This I can bear   This I cannot bear
   with another.   with another.

   ___________________   ___________________

   ___________________   ___________________

   ___________________   ___________________

CONFER: *Guide questions for discussion*

1. What makes us escape from helping one another?

2. What reasons can you give to explain why we "detour" or have the "seem I never saw" attitude when we pass by someone who is in need?

3. Why are people impatient to help the unfortunate?

4. Are we obliged to bear one another even if we cannot afford to? Are there limitations to helping?

5. Are we supposed to be selective in bearing one another?

Bear One Another

Bear one another... Galatians 6:2 NIV

"HELP," groaned a suffering man slumped in the middle of the street. While was on his way to the city, he was robbed and left half-dead. Moments later, an indifferent high-ranking spiritual leader passed him by chance. Dressed in his best designer suit, he was riding in his brand-new limousine. He stopped, took one look at the unfortunate man, and went on his way. Maybe he was busy or hurrying to a council meeting or a religious service.

A second man happened to pass by; a spiritual man, a man called by God as His child, a man, Jesus saved, and died for in Calvary. He is also an officer of their church, riding his secondhand car, a Christian saw the half-dead man. He also did not stop to help perhaps, he has been helping a lot in the church, "No, not another sacrifice," he is going to a crusade where a crowd is waiting. He too passed another way.

Then a poor man came, one rejected in the society of the "can afford" and "high class." A member of the poor class often ignored at the end of the pews. He saw and took the victim. The poor man in eagerness to help even forgot where he would get his next meal. Sacrificing his time, money, he did not attend to his important appointment that when missed would leave his family hungry. He took the opportunity in giving all he can to a man he never knew, a total stranger to him.

To bear means to help, to assist, it could also mean to be patient to those who are weak, failing, disabled, uneducated and stubborn. Bishop Westcott preached, "What we can do for another is the best of power; what we can suffer for, is a test of love". John Ruskin comments "He who serves his brother best bets nearer to God than all the rest".

Eleanor Roosevelt's observation was right, she said, "We are

Marvin Marcelino

afraid to care too much, for fear that the other person does not care at all." "To communicate," noted William Munford, "is sometimes more than to give, for money is external than man's self, but he who bestows compassion communicates his own soul." Henry Ward Beecher counsels, "to be full of goodness, full of cheerfulness, full of sympathy, full of help, full of hope causes a man to carry blessing of which he is unconscious as a lamp of its shining."

Even the wisest king has a lot to say about bearing one another, he said, "happy is he who is kind to the poor" (Proverbs 14:21). "The generous are blessed" (Proverbs 22:9), for riches are a blessing entirely to those who make them a blessing also to others, it is a good exercise for one's heart to bend and help another up!

"No matter how high the profession one possesses, he whose heart is not filled with the love of God and his fellowmen is not a true disciple of Christ. Though he should posse's great faith and has power even to work miracle, yet without love his faith is worthless. He might display great liberality; but should he from some other motive than genuine love, bestow all his goods to feed the poor, the act would not commend him to the favor of God."34

"The spirit of unselfish labor for others gives depth, stability, and Christ like loveliness to the character."35

Have you been helping one another?

HOW TO BEAR ONE ANOTHER

- ❑ Help the weak, be patient (1Thessalonians 5:14).
- ❑ Bear the infirmities of the weak (Romans 15:1).
- ❑ Do help in secret (Matthew 6:3).
- ❑ Blessed are the merciful (Matthew 5:7).
- ❑ Blessed are the meek (Matthew 5:5).
- ❑ The Generous are blessed (Proverbs 22:9).
- ❑ Say to everyone, "Brother, take courage" (Isaiah 41:6).
- ❑ Be happy and kind to the poor (Proverbs 14:21).
- ❑ Love you neighbor as yourself (Leviticus 19:18).
- ❑ Be a servant; serve like a slave (Mark 10:44).
- ❑ Remember you are to serve not to be served (Mark 10:44).
- ❑ Whatever spiritual gift you have share by serving.
- ❑ Help made secret are rewarded (Matthew 6:4).

PRAYER

Dear Heavenly Father, I confess that most of the time I do not help ______________. Teach me Father, Jesus has been very helpful to me a sinner, yet he bears my burdens. I beg the Holy Spirit to create in me a clean and new heart that I may help those in need. This I pray in the name of Jesus Christ my Lord. Amen.

AFFIRMATION

I am a channel of God's love. I am to bear another's weaknesses and help others in times of their need, with my money or my time even if I cannot afford to do so.

Marvin Marcelino

Forgiving is letting what was, be gone.
What will be, come; what is now, be.
DAVID AUSBERG

When we forgive, we free ourselves from bitter ties
that bind us to the one who hurt us.
CLAIRE FRAZIER YZAGUIRRE

Forgive One Another

UTMOST PARDON
Complete the sentences.
1. Forgiving to me means...

____

Supply names of your acquaintances.

2. Who has forgiven me?

____

____

3. Whom have I forgiven?

____

____

4. Who has not forgiven me?

____

____

5. Whom will I not forgive?

____

____

CONFRONT: Guide questions for discussion

1. 1.What does it take for a human to forgive another?

2. What hinders one in forgiving another?

3. What makes a man noble according to Leo Baeck? Explain.

4. Why is remembering the past said to be a sign of not having forgiven?

5. Have you really forgiven one another? How did you do it?

6. When letting go of a hurt, what percent of the hurt remains?

Marvin Marcelino

Forgive One Another

Forgive one another...   Colossians 3:13 NIV

have been insulted!" A young man said in the village as he hurried to his pastor to tell him about it. He swore to avenge his honor. "Better go home son," said the pastor kindly. "But I've been insulted!" The young man repeated. "That's exactly why you should go home," "An insult," said the pastor, "is like mud," "I knew that, and I'm going to clean it up," battled the young man. "Son, there is one thing you might as well learn now. "Mud brushes off a lot easier, when it is dry."36

Leo Baeck urged that the true test of a man is to create a noble memory, a mind filled with forgiveness." Ellen White counsels, "One of the most common sins, and one with the most pernicious result is the indulgence of an unforgiving spirit... We are dependent upon the pardoning mercy of God... every day and every hour; how they can cherish bitterness and malice toward our fellow sinners if in all their darting discourse. Christians should carry out the principles of this prayer, what a blessed change would be wrought in the church, and on the world, this would be most convincing testimony that would be given to the reality of the religion of the Bible."37

So many people go through life filling their minds with the miscellaneous items of grudges, a jealousy, bitterness, and selfishness - all ignoble. "Anger," Lowell Fillmore alludes, "is a thief that seizes and controls a person's mind and uses them blindly and destructively".

Issue of Reader's Digest April 1990 article entitled "Your Anger Can Kill You," suggests eight steps to control anger – Step number seven said Practice forgiving by letting go of resentment and retribution. You may find that the weight of anger lifts from your shoulders and helps you forget the wrong.

Louie Ten Boon in his book *Hiding Place* said, "If people can be taught to hate, they can be taught to love. We must find a way, no matter how long it takes to love." Forgiveness is the key to freedom from resentment. Since we all need forgiveness, we also should be forgiving. "We are not forgiven because we do not forgive; but as we forgive the ground of all forgiveness is found in the unmerited love of God, but our attitude toward others we shun whether we have made that love our own."38

John 8:3-11 records an incident of socially convicted person, Jesus exemplifies what we ought to be doing. Let us comfort them, accept without condemnation, and forgive with unconditional love. Proverb 25:21 even suggest that we feed our enemy.

In the book *Love, Acceptance and Forgiveness*, Jerry Cook suggested three guarantees to an offender. 1) That under all circumstances without exception, the offender feels loved. 2) They will have unconditional acceptance. 3) No matter how many times they failed, unreserved forgiveness is for them with no bitter memory. When it seems you cannot forgive, remember how much God has forgiven you. Mahatma Gandhi posed this to ponder upon, "The weak can never forgive. Forgiveness is the attribute of the strong."

Forgiveness is costly. Our forgiveness made possible by Christ's cross. We would have no forgiveness without His pain and suffering. Forgiveness does not naturally come it is taught. "Forgive anyone so that your Father in heaven can forgive you"(Mark 11:25). "If a man sins against another man; God will mediate" (1Samuel 2:25). "If you have given offense to your friend or neighbor you are to acknowledge your wrong, and it is his duty to forgive you. Then you are to seek the forgiveness of God because the brother you have wounded is God's property, and in injuring him, you are sinning against His creator and redeemer."39

C. S. Lewis concludes, "To be a Christian means to forgive the inexcusable because God has forgiven the inexcusable in you." An unknown author adds, "That forgiveness is the first gift of God's grace to us through Christ, it is the duty which the Christian owes to his fellow men."

Have you REALLY forgiven one another?

Marvin Marcelino

HOW TO FORGIVE ONE ANOTHER

- ❏ Forgive that your Father in heaven may forgive you (Matthew 18:35).
- ❏ We should not hate our brothers in our hearts (Leviticus 19:17,18).
- ❏ Be forgiving (Ephesians 4:32).
- ❏ Be merciful (Matthew 5:7).
- ❏ Love your neighbor and do good to them that hate you (Luke 6:27).
- ❏ Be patient and kind (1Corinthians 13:4).
- ❏ Bless those who curse you (Matthew 5:44).
- ❏ Pray for them that abase you.
- ❏ If you cannot forgive, remember how God has forgiven you.
- ❏ Forget the former things and do not dwell on them (Isaiah 43:18).
- ❏ Forgive many times (Matthew 17:7).
- ❏ Forgive 70x7 (Matthew 18:22).
- ❏ Forgive your brothers from the HEART! (Matthew 18:33-35)
- ❏ Let go off all the pain inside.

PRAYER

Dear Heavenly Father, I admit that I have not forgiven _________________. Teach me, Father, the kind of forgiveness you bestow to me, a sinner. I beg the Holy Spirit to cleanse my heart from self-centeredness and pain for I am to be forgiving. This I pray in the name of Jesus Christ, my Lord. Amen.

AFFIRMATION

I am letting go of all the hurts I have been keeping inside of me for I am a child of Peace. God has spent so much for my forgiveness, and I am to forgive others as He forgives me.

His [Jesus] heart was as great as the world,
but there was no room in it to
hold the memory of a wrong.
RALPH WALDO EMERSON

Speak no evil, hear no evil, talk no evil.
CHINESE PROVERB

Slander Not One Another

BACKSLASHER
Choose and check three only.

1. If I would comment on my slandering, I would say...

[] it is addictive.

[] it is just for getting even

[] it is revenge.

[] it is just a habit

[] I never knew it is a sin!

[] it is my favorite pastime.

[] I cannot get rid of it.

[] please cut my tongue.

[] I need revival.

[] pray for me.

[] something I need help on

[] I just do not care about it.

2. Give reasons for your chosen answers.

____

____

1. What is slandering? Give some examples.

2. Have you been a victim of slander? How did you feel?

3. How can we avoid the sin of slandering?

4. How should we treat somebody who spreads slander?

5. What would you do if you learned someone was spreading false reports about you? Read Psalms 41:5.

6. What is our best protection against slander?

Slander Not One Another

Slander not one another... James 4:11 NIV

H e sexually harassed me!" cried a beautiful middle aged rich woman, as she faced the investigators. As reporters and media, people found a spot to get most of the issue. The accused continually denied the accusation. The woman was the wife of a rich, influential, political leader, a high-ranking official of the Egyptian government. The suspect was a poor houseboy, a young and handsome Hebrew. The incident made it to the headlines of the newspapers, TV, and radio with the title: "Governor's wife raped, suspect nabbed!" (Genesis 39)

God hates slanderers. They are scoundrels and villains with hidden hatred in their hearts, devils in their mouths. Some people have turned slander into a fine art. They would never use a meat cutter to cut down another person. They are shrewder. They have learned to slander with a gesture, a wink, or a wicked smile.

Jonathan Swift conveys, "A libel can be made in a frown and a wink and can put reputation down." "It is better to be good and appear foolish than to open your mouth and remove all doubt," because when you throw mud, you are always left with dirt in your hands."

A famous author wrote, "While slander may blacken your reputation it cannot stain the character." That is in God's keeping. So long as we do not consent to sin, there is no power, whether human or satanic, that can bring a stain to the soul. A man whose heart stayed is upon God are just the same in the hour of his most afflicting trials and most discouraging surrounding as when he is in prosperity. When the light and favor of God seems to be upon him, his words, his nature, he is falsified, but he does not mind it because he has a greater interest at stake."40

The Wise King was right when he wrote, "You can win more friends with your ears than with your mouth" (Proverbs 17:28). A great slanderer is a fool (Proverbs 10:18). He destroys others; he winks, motions, or gives a shrug to work slander. After all, it is

Marvin Marcelino

difficult to refute a gesture or to prove evil in a wink. His actions are subtle but are deadly as bullets piercing the heart. In the book *Basic Christianity* by J R W Stolt, it states, "All forms of scandal and slander, all idle talk and tittles tattle, all lies are deliberate exaggerations or distortions of truth." "We can listen to unkind rumor, as well as pass them on by telling jokes at somebody else's expense, by creating a false impression, by not correcting untrue statements, and by our silence as well as our speech."

"Let no evil talk come out of your mouths, but only such is good for edifying as fit the occasions that it may impart grace to those who hear. Moreover, do not grieve the Holy Spirit of God, in whom you were sealed for the day of redemption. Let all bitterness and wrath and anger and clamor and slander be put away from you, with all malice and be kind to one another as God in Christ forgave you"(Ephesians 4:29-32). If we have not turned our tongue over to God, we have surrendered it for Satan's use.

For "whoever spread slanders is a fool" (Proverbs 10:18). Argue your case with your neighbor himself, not with others and do not tell another's secret (Proverbs 29:5). Be careful with your tongue because it is always on the wet place and can easily slip. Jeremy Taylor adds, "In the use of the tongue, God distinguishes us from the beast and by the will and its use we are distinguished from one another."

Noah Webster laid down a rule; we should say nothing of a person in his absence and that we should be willing to say it if he or she is present. The Lord knows all the words of our mouth (Psalms 139:4). Rebuke those who backbite (Proverbs 25:23). Let peace, gentleness, mercy, good fruits, impartiality, and transparency dominate. Allow the fruit of righteousness be sown to make peace (James 3:13-18).

Have you been slandering one another?

HOW NOT TO SLANDER ONE ANOTHER

- ❑ We should not hate our brothers in our hearts (Leviticus 19:17, 18).
- ❑ Be forgiving (Ephesians 4:32).
- ❑ Be merciful (Matthew 5:7).
- ❑ Remember that "he who slanders his neighbor...I (God) will destroy" (Psalms 101:5).
- ❑ Do not speak falsely about your neighbor (Exodus 20:16).
- ❑ Do not kill (Exodus 20:13).
- ❑ Do not be envious of your neighbor's goods (Exo. 20:17).
- ❑ Be peacemakers (Matthew 5:9).
- ❑ Be kind to those who are unkind to you (Luke 6:35).
- ❑ Be careful with your words because you are accountable for them on the judgment day (Matthew 12:36, 39).
- ❑ Put away all evil communication and bitterness (Eph. 3:8, 31).
- ❑ Do not tell lies.
- ❑ Remember that a slanderer is a fool (Proverbs 10:18).
- ❑ Do not associate with one who speaks foolishness (Prov. 20:19).
- ❑ Do not listen to wicked lips (Proverbs 17:4).
- ❑ Let all conversation be without covetousness (Hebrews13: 5).
- ❑ Do not hate your brother (1John2:9).
- ❑ Say nothing about a person in his absence.

PRAYER

Dear Heavenly Father, I confess that I am guilty of slandering against _______________. Help me, Father, to overcome this bad habit. I beg the Holy Spirit to guard my lips and ears against false reports about other people for I am supposed to speak love. This I pray in the name of Jesus Christ, my Lord and Savior. Amen.

AFFIRMATION

I am a new creation in Christ and my words are only of loving, pure and acceptable in God's sight. I only see the good in others for I am a peacemaker.

Marvin Marcelino

The devil can cite scripture for his purpose.
WILLIAM SHAKESPEARE

One evil does not correct another evil.
JOSE P. RIZAL

Devise No Evil Against One Another

GRIM SCHEMER
Choose and check three.

1. Whenever I think evil against my neighbor...

▢ It is addictive	▢ It gives me joy.
▢ It is revenge	▢ I need someone to stop me.
▢ It's just a habit	▢ Pray for me.
▢ I never knew it is a sin!	▢ Something I need help on
▢ It is my favorite pastime	▢ I do not care.
▢ It is irresistible	▢ I cannot get rid of it.

2. Why?

____

CONFER: *Guide questions for discussion*

1.   What triggers one to devise evil against another?

2.   What should one do if he learns that someone is planning evil against another?

3.   Why do we always need to subject our mind to reason?

4.   What would you do to fight off the temptation of devising evil against another?

5.   How is hating alone considered murder?

Marvin Marcelino

Devise No Evil Against One Another

*Devise no evil in your hearts against
one another... Zechariah 8:17 NIV*

Evil acts begin with evil thoughts. Lucifer did it in the Garden of Eden. Simeon and Levi did it to Joseph. Sanballat, Tovia, and Gershem did it to Nehemiah, David to Uriah and the list goes on. Let us go over the text again, "Devise no evil in your hearts against one another..." is not that a brilliant advice from God? We do not stop there; let us continue the last part of the verse: "for all these things I hate says the Lord" (Zechariah 8:17).

In 1996, I worked as an instructor at the Philippine National Police Academy, where I taught the subject criminal behavior. In one of the classrooms, a phrase that caught my eyes, it says, "Crime starts in the mind." True to the saying, immoral behavior starts in the mind through the power of darkness.

A famous author, Ellen White wrote, "The sin of evil speaking begins with the cherishing of evil thoughts. Guile induces impurity in all forms. An impure thought tolerated as unholy desire cherished, and the soul is contaminated, its integrity compromised. Then when lust hath conceived, it brings forth sin; and sin when it is finished, brings forth death, if we would not commit sin, we must shun its very beginnings. Every emotion and desire held up in subjection to reason and conscience. Every unholy thought must be instantly repelled."41

"Think one noble thought that does not come from God...Intellect ennobled, purified; heaven directed is the universal power to build up the kingdom of God. Intellect perverted has exactly the opposite influences. It is corrupting of the given human power, where trust is multiplied in earnest labor for good."42

We must admit that we all have a tendency to be deceitful. We deceive by wearing a mask of deception, and flattering, winking at wrong, or saying just trying to be diplomatic. When we do these, we are undoubtedly following the example of the Devil - the Father of Lies (John 8:44). "How often," Margaret E Bruner said, "for some trivial wrong, in anger we retaliate."

It takes too long for us to learn that life is far too brief for hate. "Must not hate thy brother in your heart... you must not avenge or keep any grudges against the children of thy people, but you must love your neighbor as yourself"(Leviticus 19:17, 18). Ellen White counsels, "The spirit of hate and revenge originated with Satan, and it led him put to death the Son of God. Whoever cherishes malice or unkindness is cherishing the same spirit and its fruits will be unto death. His vengeful thoughts, the evil deeds he enfolded, as the plant in the seed. "Whosoever hates his brother is a murderer and ye know that no murderer hath eternal life abiding him (1John 3:15)."43 "For the spirit that we manifest toward our fellow declares our spirit toward God in the heart and is the only source of love toward our neighbor."44

See what the Bible says to those who will do evil, "You must purge evil away from you (Deuteronomy 17:7), or any likeness of it. (Job 22:23) Expel evil (1Corinthians 5:13) for God will bring terror and disease upon you (Leviticus 26:16) and be swept away and destroyed. (Isaiah 12:25) You will be ill-treated, (Isaiah 66:4) and God will testify against you" (Malachi 3:5).

A story once told about a frog that had a tricky idea. He tied the rat's foot to his own, and off they went in search for food. Eventually they came onto a shore by the lake; the frog dived in shouting, "Croak, croak, croak." and dragged the rat after him. The unfortunate drowned and his corpse rose to the surface still tied to the frog's foot. A crow saw what happened and swooped down and seized the body of the rat in his talons, carrying it along with the helpless frog that would now form part of the crow's supper."45

Indeed, evil thoughts and deeds have its own way to where it originated. As Lucius Annaeus Seneca did say, "He that does good to another does good to himself."

Have you been devising evil against another?

HOW NOT TO DEVISE EVIL TO ONE ANOTHER

- ❏ Do not hate your brothers in your hearts (Leviticus 19:17,18).
- ❏ Bring every thought into to obedience with Christ (2Corinthians. 10:5).
- ❏ Repent, pray to God for your evil thoughts to be forgiven (Acts 8:22).
- ❏ Forgive, so that your Father in heaven can forgive you. (Mark 11:25)
- ❏ Do not plot evil because it is a sin (Proverbs 24:8,9).
- ❏ Do not kill (Exodus 20:13)
- ❏ Remember, if you hate your brother, you are a murderer (1John 3:15).
- ❏ Be a peacemaker (Matthew 5:9).
- ❏ Remember, nothing secret that will not be revealed (Luke 8:17).
- ❏ Put in mind that God knows every secret of the heart (Psalms 44:21).
- ❏ Remember deceit is in the heart of those who devise evil (Proverbs 12:20).
- ❏ Do not plan evil against your neighbors (Psalms 37:12).
- ❏ Remember a perverse man is an abomination to the Lord (Proverbs 3:32).
- ❏ Do not allow evil thoughts lodge in your mind? (Jeremiah 4:14)
- ❏ Do not render evil for evil (1Peter 3:9).
- ❏ Remember those who do evil hates the light (John 3:20).

PRAYER

Dear Heavenly Father, I confess that at times I am tempted to meditate evil against ______________. Help me Father to overcome this bad habit of devising evil against another. I beg the Holy Spirit to give me a new and clean heart and a loving spirit for I am a channel of love and not of darkness, this, I pray in the name of Jesus Christ, my Lord and Savior. Amen.

AFFIRMATION

I am a new creation in Christ and my mind is filled with love, gentleness, meekness, long-suffering, and righteousness. I am manifesting this love to others for I am a child of God.

Tell the truth, the whole truth
and nothing but the truth.
LEGAL OATH

There are some people who always
feel themselves attacked,
whenever a general truth is given.
CHRISTIAN MORGENSTEN

Speak The Truth To One Another

CONFRONT:

BLIND CANDOR
Check among the choices.

1.My habit of not speaking the truth is...

☐ Addictive
☐ My way out of trouble
☐ Revenge
☐ Just a habit
☐ Never knew it is a sin!
☐ My favorite pastime

☐ Caused by my fear
☐ To win favor.
☐ Way out of control
☐ Terrible please pray for me
☐ Something I need help on
☐ To avoid misunderstanding.

2. I speak the truth when...

____

3. I do not speak the truth when...

____

CONFER: Guide questions for discussion

1. What should be our guide in speaking the truth to another?

2. What reasons can you think that explain why it is hard for someone to tell the truth to another?

3. Why is lying an abomination (terrible sin) to the Lord?

4. How can our tongue ruin our soul?

5. If one is a liar, how is he related to Satan? Check John 8:44.

6. When somebody is silent is that considered lying?

Speak The Truth To One Another

Speak the truth to one another... Zechariah 8:16 RSV

All the troubles of the world began with one lie (John 8:44-47). Proverbs 16:12 tells us that Kings take pleasure in honest lips they value a man who speaks the truth. Paul advised us to "speak the truth with his neighbors" (Ephesians 4:25).

The ninth commandment forbids purposeful deceits against one's neighbors, and it underscores the sacredness of truth in all dealings. The Hebrew words "*shav*" in Exodus 20:16 and in Deuteronomy 5:20 mean "untrue" and "insincere." Therefore, bearing false witness against one's neighbor is an expression of insincerity and untruthfulness. "How prone are we to lying which in a stroke of exaggeration here and an omitted dot there is a misleading silence," said Robert Louis Stevenson.

Not revealing or holding the truth back is rampant in all corners of the world. A magazine reports that many celebrities never use the products they endorse. Media would not tell authorities where rebels and terrorist hide. Some producers will tell you otherwise than a poor product.

Language is a boon, and the words of human beings can be a mighty blessing. Notice the powerful rhetoric of the famous orators that can captivate an audience. Just as literary geniuses and poets can employ words of their mother tongue to stir strong emotions of love, piety or patriotism even at the expense of truth, justice and liberty.

The cruelest lies often are told in silence or distorted truths. "Truth is the superstructure of all relationship. Remove the girdle of truth and socially society will crumble. Many among us do not

Marvin Marcelino

frankly speak the truth before man indirectly we tell and pass the truth to another than the person involved, which for a time will eventually reach its destiny.

All of us have different attitudes towards truth and each of us react differently. To some, according to Nicholas Humphrey, "speaking the truth to the people who do not want to hear it is considered almost an aggressive act, an invasion to privacy, a trespass into someone else's space." Yes, the truth hurts.

Are your words pure and free of lies? The word 'sound' used in 2Timothy 1:13, is translated from the Greek word which has been adapted into English as "hygiene." It implies health and life as opposed to disease and death. It implies purity of expressions and implies words that heal, encourages, and uplifts the broken hearted, bring solace to the sad, give hope to the depressed and the dying.

The story of salvation comes through "sound speech" that cannot be condemned Certainly pleasant words are as honeycomb, sweet to the soul, (Titus 2:8) and "health to the bones" (Proverbs 16:24).

Jesus laid down a principle that makes unnecessary oath taking. He taught that the exact truth should be "let your yes be yes, and No, no and whatsoever is ever more than this is of the evil one (Matthew 5:37). Meaning if it is black then say it is black or if its white then let it be white, no room for gray areas.

Some people say, 'yes' while they mean 'no'. Some cannot say 'no' upfront because of a favor or debt of gratitude to the person. Some avoid offending the recipient of the 'no' to a request by making them wait. Many cannot say 'no' because of fear, of rejection, or misunderstanding. It is a matter of yes or no, and the question seems easy, but the implication is hard to weigh, especially if one is after his own good rather than what is morally right.

"Deception in every one of its myriad forms is of Satan. God condemns all meaningless phrases and expletives that border in profanity. Let us condemn the deceptive compliments, the evasions of truth, the flattering phrases, the exaggerations, the misrepresentations in a trade that are current in society. Let us teach that any words that do not convey the real sentiments of his heart are not telling the truth. Everyday Christians should be as transparent as the sunlight because Truth is of God."

"Stand in defense of truth and righteousness when the majority forsake us...this will be our best test."46 "If you keep or bury the truth under the ground; it will grow and gather to itself such explosive power until the day it burst through," warns Emily Zola, "it will blow up everything on its way."

David's excellent prayer was "Guard O Lord my mouth keep watch over the door of my lips (Psalms 141:3). Proverbs 12:17-22 guide us not to sin. As a line in a hymn, "Take my lips and let them be filled with messages from thee."

Have you been speaking the truth to one another?

COMMIT:

HOW TO SPEAK THE TRUTH TO ONE ANOTHER

❏Nothing is secret that will not be revealed. (Luke 8:17)
❏God knows every secret of the heart. (Psalms 44:21)
❏Do my lips utter my own words, or they are guided by God? (Psalm 19:14)
❏Do not lie to each other. (Colossian 3:9)
❏Remember, "Your tongue can defile all your body. (Jas 3:6)
❏May this be your watch word -WATCH YOUR WORD
❏You can get caught by the word with a hook.
❏Your speech must be found with no guile. (Proverbs 14:5)
❏Remember idle words will give account on judgment day. (Matthew 12:36)
❏Do not bear false witness. (Exodus 20:16)
❏Speak the truth and your righteousness is seen. (Proverbs 12:17)
❏Truth last forever but lies is but a moment (Proverbs 12:19)
❏Lying lips are an abomination to the Lord. (Proverbs 12:22)
❏May the Lord cut all flattering lips (Psalms 12:3)
❏Give honest evidence. (Proverbs 14:5; 12:17)
❏Tell the truth in love. (Ephesians 4:15)

PRAYER

Dear Heavenly Father, I admit that I have lied to _____________, because I am more concerned with my _____________. Teach me Father to speak the truth, the whole truth and nothing but truth only. Give me the clarity and courage of Jesus who spoke nothing but truth. I beg the Holy Spirit to cleanse my lips of lies. This I pray in the name of Jesus Christ, my Lord and Savior. Amen.

AFFIRMATION

I am only to speak the truth without fear and favor. Christ died for me so that truth might be established. My words are always pure, and acceptable before God.

Love that leads to life is the noblest.
HARRY VAN DYKE

Sanctified love for one another
is sacred in the great work.
ELLEN G. WHITE

Love One Another

LOVER'S LANE
Fill in with names of people you daily encounter.

1. This is the persons I...

Love best _________________ because _________________.
Love less _________________ because _________________.
Love least _________________ because _________________.
Love not _________________ because _________________.
Love worst _________________ because _________________.
Will never love _____________ because _________________.

CONFER: *Guide questions for discussion*

1. What hinders you to love right? Give some reasons.

2. What reasons can you think of that hinder others to love you?

3. With whom do you think you need to be loving with?

4. How can we truly follow the way a true Christian should love?

5. After studying this chapter, how do you rate the way you love? From a scale of 1-10 (Ten being the highest)

Love One Another

Love one another... 1 John 3:11 NIV

A Child psychologist spent many hours constructing a new driveway at his home. Just right after he smoothed the surface of the freshly paved concrete, his small children chased a ball across the driveway leaving deep footprints. The man yelled after them with a torrent of angry words. His shocked wife said, "You're a psychologist who is supposed to love children." The fuming man shouted, "I love children in the abstract, not in the concrete!"47

Love is an action word. Love is an active participle that is continuous and genuine. Do we ask why we need to love? To Dryden, "Love is a passion that kindles honor into noble acts." Eric Hoffer adds, "It's easier to love humanity as a whole than to love one's neighbor."

For me, the most important reason is that God first loved us (1John 4:19), and men that do not love, do not know God (1John 4:8). How? Simple, before man, God was. God originated and came to teach us His precepts. As written the God of love is our Father, then, you and I are children of Him who is love. If we are children of love then we do know God, and if we do not love then we do not know God, then we are atheist- a people prejudice to God and His people.

The key question is why there exists a counterfeit love opposed to a genuine love. As it is written, in the last days many will hate one another (Matthew 24:10, 12). "The true spirit of a man is manifested by how he deals with his fellow man. We may ask the question, does he represent the character of Christ in spirit and action, or simply manifest the natural, selfish traits of a character that belongs to the people of this world if he is then professing to be a Christian weigh nothing to God."48

According to Harry Van Dyke, "There are many kinds of

Marvin Marcelino

love as there is light; every kind of love makes a glory in the night. There is love that stirs the heart, love that gives rest. But the love that leads life upward is the noblest and the best." People express their love in four ways: 1)"I want you; therefore, I love you" (A self-seeking love). 2)"I need you; therefore, I love you" (This is demanding and conditional love). 3)"You need me; therefore, I love you" (Requires loving self before sharing himself to another). 4) "I love you; no matter what" (Love accepts even before we will love each other and open ourselves with one another).

"The deepest desire of any individual is to love and be loved," according to Earne Larsen. To be happy, we need to love and loving which makes us healthy. As we acquire health then love makes us different.

"Let love be genuine, shone what is evil, hold fast to what is good, love one another with brotherly affection." "A new commandment I give unto you that you love one another; I have loved you that you love one another" (John 13:34-35). By that shall all men know that you are my disciple if you love one another.

Send out thought after thought, kindness after kindness, forgiveness after forgiveness as you weave a chain of love, which nothing can break. See how God can bring the erring one to His open heart! Truly, there comes a time when your loved ones will not seem to care. There is only one thing to do, keep on loving! To Pastor Jaime Castrero, "Loving one another is not only a duty for Christians, our Lord made it a seal mark of discipleship itself: (By these shall all men know)".

Ellen White commented, "Sanctified love for one another is sacred in the great work, Christian love for another...preserves Christian benevolence and politeness and enfolds human brotherhood in the embrace of God."49 Lastly, Bern William wrote, "Love is a straight line. It goes directly to the loved one. Hate is a circle; it eventually comes back to the hater." Ellen White said, "Love is a golden chain that binds believing hearts to one another and to God."50

Saint Augustine of Hippo's students asked him, "What does love look like?" The teacher answered this; "It has hands to help others. It has feet to hasten to the poor and needy. It has eyes to see the misery and need. It has ears to hear the sigh and sorrows of men. That is what love looks like." Do you love all the time?

Marvin Marcelino

HOW TO LOVE ONE ANOTHER

- ❑ Love to know love (1John 4:8).
- ❑ Aim to touch the heart of God by loving even the unbearable.
- ❑ Have a heart for God to have a heart for people,
- ❑ Remember people we like least may need our love most.
- ❑ Do well to all (Galatians 6:10).
- ❑ Be active- love is an active word.
- ❑ Do not love in speech but in deed and in truth (1John 3:18).
- ❑ Love each other as Jesus loves us (John 15:12).
- ❑ Do not hate because it is the same as murder with the hand (Matthew 5:21,22).
- ❑ Be a disciple of Jesus (John 13:34, 35).
- ❑ Do LOVE (1Corinthians 13:2).
- ❑ Love your neighbor as you love yourself (Matthew 22:36-40).
- ❑ Make your love be genuine, hate what is evil (Romans 12:9).
- ❑ Love one another (Romans 12:10).
- ❑ Do keep brotherly love continue (Hebrews 13:1).

PRAYER

Dear Heavenly Father, I admit that I really do not offer agape love to ______________. Teach me Father to love the way You love me, even though I am a sinner, you love me unconditionally. I beg the Holy Spirit to lead me to the way of Agape love. This I pray in the name of Jesus Christ, my Lord and Savior. Amen.

AFFIRMATION

I exist because of the love of God, and I am here to love others.

It seems to me that people should be
impatient only with themselves,
and not with others.
HERMAN HESSE

The kindest and the happiest pair
will find occasion to forbear...they live
to pity and perhaps forgive.
WILLIAM COWPER

Marvin Marcelino

Forbear One Another

PATIENCE THRESHOLD TEST
List things you cannot be patient within other people.

1. Unbearable   Moderately Bearable   Bearable

_______________   _______________   _______________
_______________   _______________   _______________
_______________   _______________   _______________
_______________   _______________   _______________

2. Why do you think you need to have Christ like patience?

_______________   _______________   _______________
_______________   _______________   _______________

CONFER: Guide questions for discussion

1. What are the things that cut your patience short? (Things you are impatient with.) Give a few examples and state the reasons why.

2. How do you express yourself when you are impatient?

3. What characteristics do you have that hinders others to be forbearing or patient with you?

4. How can you change to be more forbearing, longsuffering, and patient?

5. Is your being impatient expressing love? How do you show impatience with love?

Forbear One Another

**With lowliness, with meekness, longsuffering
forbear one another. Ephesians 4:2RSV**

Two neighbors who have a lifetime dispute met again. One got very sick and almost died, a pastor was called to reconcile the two before death. Both agreed to let forgive and forget their past quarrels. Everything went well they cried and embraced one another. As the other was leaving, the dying raised is fist and sharply said, "This only counts in case I die!51

"Patience is the best remedy for every trouble," said Publius Syrus. This is what Proverbs 16:32 is trying to convey, "A man of understanding is even tempered." In addition, we are not to fret because we are not evil man (Proverbs 24:19).

Dr. John Schindler in his book *How to Live 365 Days a Year* said, "Did you not know that emotional stress is the number one cause of ill health? More than fifty percent of all medical problems are emotionally induced... but by simply understanding and controlling our feelings, your chances for a healthier, happier longer life are automatically increased... because of anger the inner portion of the medulla of the adrenaline glands releases chemicals known as the **catecholamines,** which rate your temper. This increases the heart rate, elevates blood pressure, and raises the level of free fatty acids in the blood. This may lead to migraines, hypertension, coronary heart diseases and strokes."

To love is to forbear or to be patient. To forbear means, avoid, withhold, abstain, keep, compassionate, tolerance, and acceptance. Enter the sublime patience of the Lord. Be considerate in view of it.

God keeps His patience on us, why we cannot with one another. Let patience have its perfect work bring forth her celestial fruits. "Though the Lord be high, yet hath he respects to the lowly" (Psalms 138:6). "Man is to represent Christ. He is to be

Marvin Marcelino

longsuffering toward his fellowmen, to be patient, forgiving and full of Christ-like love. He who is fully converted will manifest respect for his brethren."52

Patience works wonders like the drip of water to the hard cement floor that, for a time was able to make a hole in the floor it. Patience comes only from the mind that is calm, not reactive, a mind that is controlled by inner peace and power of the will and not by the wheel of events. Patience works as a sponge, to absorb the impact of negative forces and turn them to positive responses that work for both you and others. This is the Aikido of love.

Is it a surprise when others treat us with gentleness since we live in a world of aggression and sarcasm? "Human nature is ever struggling for expression for contest, but he who learns of Christ is emptied of self, of pride, of love of supremacy, and there is silence in the soul. Self yields to the disposal of the Holy Spirit. Then we are not anxious to have the highest place. We have no ambition to crowd and elbow others into notices, but we feel that our highest place is at the feet of our Savior."53

Meekness is Christlikeness, a virtue every Christian should seek and cultivate, for the meek will inherit the kingdom of God (Numbers 12:3). "If we could humble ourselves before God and be kind and courteous and tenderhearted and pitiful, there would be one hundred conversions to the truth, where now there is only one."54

Notice in these last days we need to triple our patience, in Filipino we would say, "We need to lengthen our shoelace," "for many will be more subtle, stubborn and self-serving (2Timothy 3:1-9). I like the Chinese proverb that says, "Be not disturbed at being misunderstood; be disturbed rather at not being understanding."

You must be strong by maintaining the unity of the spirit of love in you, by means of self-control. The greater the evil, the stronger our love must be. In application - when someone does you wrong, do not do what comes naturally, do what comes supernaturally! -LOVE him! "Love not only bears with others' fault but cheerfully submits to whatever suffering or inconvenience such forbearance makes necessary. This love never fails."55 "Christ expressed his love for his disciples. Their selfish spirit filled Him with sorrow, but he entered with no controversy with them regarding their difficulty."56

Have you been patient with one another?

HOW TO FORBEAR ONE ANOTHER

- ❑ Be peacemakers (Matthew 5:9).
- ❑ Win by patience (Luke 8:15).
- ❑ Be patient one another. Practice self-control.
- ❑ Be patient like Christ (Matthew 11:29).
- ❑ Aim to touch the heart of God by loving even the unbearable.
- ❑ Have a heart for God to have a heart for people,
- ❑ Be meek (Matthew 5:5).
- ❑ Learn from the meekest man-Moses (Numbers 12:3; Exodus 32:7-14,19-33).
- ❑ Control your emotions (cool man cool)
- ❑ Be patient like enduring the nails on the Cross-of Calvary.
- ❑ Show meekness unto all men (Titus 3:2).
- ❑ Bear the weakness of the weak (Romans 15:1).
- ❑ Endure with patience everyday (2Corinthians 6:4).
- ❑ Be patient up to the coming of the Lord (James 5:7).
- ❑ Be patient with the faults of others they too must be patient with yours.
- ❑ Love with patience and kindness (1Corinthians 13:4).

PRAYER

Dear Heavenly Father, I confess that I am not that patient with _______________. Help me Father to be more patient and longsuffering. Teach me the kind of patience Jesus shows me. I beg the Holy Spirit to guide my heart to patience, forbearance, and gentleness. This I pray in the name of Christ Jesus, my Lord and Savior. Amen.

AFFIRMATION

I am patient and longsuffering. I am not easily affected and provoked by circumstances, for the peace of God is within me and rules my heart.

Above all, we must have union,
only in that way shall we be strong.
JUAN LUNA

Brotherhood is the very price and
condition of man's survival.
CARLOS P ROMULO

All for one, one for all.
ALEXANDER DUMAS

Fellowship With One Another

CONFRONT:

THROW FELLOW

List names that have something to do with fellowship.

1. I like to fellowship with

because

____________________________   ____________________________

2. I don't like to fellowship
with...

because

____________________________   ____________________________

3. I'll never fellowship
with...

because

____________________________   ____________________________

4. Now that I understand what fellowship means, the first thing I will do is...

____

CONFER: Guide questions for discussion

1. Why fellowshipping with one another is considered very important? Give some positive outcomes.

2. How can you nurture fellowship with one another?

3. Why do people not fellowship with one another?

4. How will you overcome *"just us"* spirit in a fellowship gathering?

5. Should a Christian be choosy to whom he spends fellowship?

6. What kind of fellowship would strengthen your relationship with Christ and with others? Give some examples.

Fellowship With One Another

We have fellowship with one another.   1 John 1:7 RSV

An aged dying father called his seven sons around him. He gave each a stick and said, "Break it." Each easily broke his own stick. The old man then bound seven sticks into a bundle, gave it to his eldest and said, "Break it", he could not nor could any of the rest. "So," said the father, "it could be that, alone you are weak, but together you are strong.57

Carlos P. Romulo is right when he preached, "Brotherhood is the very price and condition of man's survival." Moreover, as the Hasidic proverb supports, "The man who thinks he can live without others is mistaken; the one who thinks others can live without him is even more deluded."

To love is to fellowship together. Fellowship means to be together, to share with other, to participate, to cooperate, to have the willingness to communicate, and to be part. John RW Stott comments, "Fellowship is a relational word, and it is the common participation in the grace of God, the salvation of Christ and the indwelling of the Holy Spirit which is the spiritual birthright of all believers. It is our common possession of God, Father, Son and Holy Spirit that make us one."

One classic and an exceptionally touching fellowship recorded in the Bible happened in Macedonia where sharing turned into abundance. A simple equation of joy over extreme poverty equals relief of the saints. The brethren at Macedonia came together and were able to pass through their worst crisis.

This is the typical church fellowship in the Philippines especially during times of unbearable economic crisis. The church will call for fellowship and potluck. Meager food from every home that is not even enough for the family, is brought to the potluck. By God's grace and blessings, miracle made it just enough for everybody in the church. We had a feast during crisis!

Marvin Marcelino

Today there is an urgent need to overhaul the way we fellowship. We equate fellowship with a potluck reduced to simply eating together. There is the tendency to forget the person and remember how bad the food was. Some of the fellowships I   attended are all "eat and run" event; no real fellowship took place, but a picnic. Fellowship is not all eating for physical needs!

Church fellowship's main objective is spiritual growth, renewal of commitment, strengthening of one's faith by shared spiritual adventures and experiences. Fellowship is like when you are awed because you are not alone in the truth you are holding. You sense, you witness, and you can interact with the people who realize the same truth as you have. By their experiences, you in your spiritual adventures is strengthened, encouraged, energized, become even bolder and more inspired to continue- that is fellowship.

Believers in Christ must associate together in Christian fellowship, regarding one another as brothers and sisters in the Lord. They are to love one another as Christ loves them. They are to be light for good. They are to share in the church and the world after receiving graces for grace. "These they were constantly kept as spiritual hearers of God. They reflect the image of God."58 Paul advised us to meet always until the coming of the Lord (Hebrews 10:25).

During fellowship, it is proper to meet all who have come, speak to all, get acquainted, lengthen your list of brothers and sisters in Christ, share your spiritual experience in Christ or listen to others. Both of you will surely benefit from each other's spiritual blessings.

Strengthen the spirit of fellowship within each of us - born of common trust in God and common heart with one another. The joy, which we are looking for, does not come from God alone. The fullness of joy we are looking for is within Christian fellowship. "Those who do not feel the necessity of seeking the assembly of the saints with the precious assurance that the Lord will meet them show lightly how they value the help that God provided for them."59

"Loving relationship and togetherness," said Leo Buscaglia "are made in heaven but is practiced on earth." Let us fellowship together, let us practice now here on earth, and when we are in heaven, it will be the happiest of all fellowship.

Have you been fellowshipping with one another?

Marvin Marcelino

COMMIT:

- ❑ HOW TO FELLOWSHIP WITH
- ❑ ONE ANOTHER

  - ❑ Share each other's spiritual adventures.
  - ❑ Meet as many brothers and sisters possible.
  - ❑ Remember two or more can endure hard times.
  - ❑ Fellowship with the fruitful (Ephesians 5:11).
  - ❑ Attend holy assemblies and do not miss it (Hebrews 10:25).
  - ❑ Entertain strangers (Hebrews 13:2).
  - ❑ Fellowship and share your spiritual adventures.
  - ❑ Share what you have even if it meager, the most important is being there where your presence is felt and cherished.

PRAYER

Dear Heavenly Father, I admit that I failed to genuinely fellowship with _____________. Teach me Father the kind of fellowship you have with us even though we are sinners. I beg the Holy Spirit to direct the way I am to fellowship with others. This I pray in the name of Jesus, Christ my Lord and Savior. Amen.

AFFIRMATION

I am a social being and part of the family of God. I am to share my faith with others so they can find hope and courage.

Nobody can do it for you.
RALPH CORDINER

No one will do it for you.
BEN STEIN

You must make it happen.
JOE GREENE

What Are You Waiting For Go Love One Another

Do what it says. James 1:22 NIV

There is no perfect time in doing *One Anothering*. There is only today and now. I urge you to begin your journey to greater level of better interpersonal relationship. Do not wait until everything is just right, it will never be perfect in these last days. Dorothy Day suggest that "We must lay one brick at a time, take one step at a time; we can be responsible only for the action of the present moment. But we can pray for an increase of Love in our hearts that will vitalize and transform all our individual actions."

There will be obstacles, hardships, and impossibilities; there will be trials, disappointments, discouragement, and persecution. So, what now? Get started, and each step you take, you grow more stronger, and more understanding, more caring, more loving. David Lloyd George is right, "Don't be afraid to take a big step. You can't cross a bog chasm in two small jumps."

The challenge is waiting for us to apply **One Anothering**. There is no new concept introduced here, we only came to cultivate this sleeping power of love within us. The same principal Jesus told and showed is the same we need to do to one another. Dorothy Parker simply illustrates that "Love is like a quicksilver in the hand. Leave the fingers open and it stays. Clutch it, and it darts away."

GO, do not dream, start slowly, and build up and love. Friedrich Nietzsche said, "He who would learn to fly one day must learn first to stand and walk and run and climb and dance; we cannot without trying." As an adage urge us that "the only way to start is to start, the first step is the hardest." Confucius knew this "a journey of thousand miles begins with one step." "What moves a man said Antoine de Saint Exupery is to take a step then another."

Ralph Cordiner is right, "nobody can do it for you." So is Ben Stein, "No one will do it for you and Joe Greene supports that, "you have to make it happen." William Faulkner is inspiring to say, "the man who removes a mountain begins by carrying away small stones."

I hope you have enjoyed through the principles of **One Anothering**. I hope that you have more awareness about the importance of better interpersonal relationship.

Every person you meet or relate with is a potential recipient of love and all you must do is apply **One Anothering**. Do not wait for the day to come when the risk to remain tight in a bud was more painful than the risk to blossom. Novalis Hardenberg has this in closing, "Love is the final end of the world's history, the Amen of the universe."

Thank you for sharing these pages with me. My prayer for you is that you love, love and love until all will love each other, then heaven will never be a fiction.

PRAYER

Dear Heavenly Father,
Grant us the true love for one another,
That we may be a part of those whom you have chosen and loved,
Even to all the unbelievers whom Christ died for.
Help us to understand each other, to be more patient and kinder,
That as we grow in love, we become closer to each other.

Heavenly Father,
You are a God of Love.
You know how much it takes to suffer, to pain and remain in Love.
Allow us to perfect this love especially for our dear ones,
Reminds us that without You, our love to one another can never be
perfect.

Heavenly Father,
Share us the fullness of Your love the perfection of Your character.
Plant in our hearts Your lovely nature of redemptive grace and
mercy,
That when two strange souls meet, they response to one another
with Love,
Then a little heaven of eternal glory is experienced
Amen.

AFFIRMATION

Today, I will love my neighbor for tomorrow maybe too late. God's grace and mercies will usher me through. I will not allow this day to pass without applying *One Anothering*.

AND THE GREATEST OF THEM ALL IS LOVE

Marvin A. Marcelino

No greater philosophy can ever outwit the wisdom of love.

No greater religion ever existed but the religion of Love.

No greater belief has ever been proven tacit than love.

No greater doctrine can ever replace the precepts of love.

No greater commission was given to mankind but to love God and man.

No greater duty is nobler for man to do but to love his neighbor.

No greater education can be taught than the experience of loving.

No greater extreme challenge exists than loving those who hurt and hate you.

No greater security can ever be reliable than being surrounded by love.

No greater economic crisis could bring to poverty a loving person.

No greater joy can ever be felt than the result of loving the unlovable.

No greater hope one could cherish than finding out somebody loves you.

No greater experience can one have but to love and be loved.

No greater technology can ever teach the manners Love.

No greater opportunity one could grab than the elusive moment to love.

No greater reward could match any grand prize than the consolation of love.

No greater sin is ever unpardonable by a merciful and forgiving Love.

No greater dream anybody ever aspire than to be truly loved.

No greater punishment is effective to any stubbornness but a firm love.

No greater psychological treatment could ever relieve the mind but Love.

No greater ugliness exists when viewed through the mirror of love.

No greater heroic deed can ever surpass the simple acts of love.

No greater cold apathy can ever divide us from the warmth of love.

No greater distance can ever be far that love could not reach.

No greater heights are ever too high that love could not touch.

No greater government is ever stable than the one whose foundation is love.

No greater nation can ever be stronger than a people who love each other.

No greater wealth of the entire world combined can ever buy a priceless Love.

No greater death is ever sweet than to die in the name of Love.

No greater language can ever be universal than the language of love.

No greater force can ever be stronger than the strength of love.

No greater war is ever fought than the battle of Love against sin and hate.

No greater evil is ever wicked that was not defeated by the power of Love.

No greater deity that has ever existed than the God that is Love.

No greater of all the greatest in the whole universe but Love.

Yes, and the greatest of all is LOVE.

Marvin Marcelino

I Have a Request

I have a request! I want you to write and tell me how this book has affected your life. Share me your stories and adventure with **One Anothering**.

Let me know how you made a difference because of reading this book. What new secrets have you discovered in relating to one another? What tips do you have that I can pass on to the future generations?

Do you have a favorite story, quote, and an insight about **One Anothering**? (*Biblical Guide to a Christian Interpersonal Relations*)

Please send it to me I am eager to hear from you. Thank you for participating in one another's life.

Please e-mail me at the following address.

Marvin A. Marcelino
at
marvzmarcelino@gmail.com

About the Author

Marvin A. Marcelino is a graduate of Bachelor of Art in History and Philosophy of Religion and Bachelor of Theology at Adventist University of the Philippines.

He was a former instructor in a Philippine government leadership institution.

He taught Values subjects in colleges and secondary Christian schools for some time. He is presently working in an international school in Bangkok, Thailand.

He is a frequent speaker to many youth and family camps, retreats, fellowships, seminars, and conferences. He is frequent resource person in the Philippines, Thailand, Malaysia, and Vietnam.

He is a coach, mentor, a trainer, counselor, a facilitator, a teacher, a father, and a friend to many young and adult.

He conducts seminars and training on leadership, management, human relations and youth and family matters.

He enjoys creating values-oriented activities for both youth and adult.

His other interests include reading, writing, filmmaking, photography, digital arts, swimming, painting, hiking, biking, and camping.

He is married to Jasmin Jimenez Marcelino a registered dietician. They were blest with three children, Joshua Marvin and Mayumi Jasmine and Mark Jiro.

He has written several books.

Marvin Marcelino

References

1. Ellen G. White, *Testimonies to the Church Vol. 8*, (Mountain View, CA: Pacific Press Publishing Association, 1948), p. 240.

2. __________, *Ye Shall Receive Power*, (Hagerstown, MD: Review and Herald Publishing Association, 1995), p. 121.

3. Dorothy Nolte as quoted by Delba de Chavez, *Learning is Fun (So Is Teaching)*, (San Pablo City: 1999) p. 34.

4. Ellen G. White, *Child Guidance*, (Mountain View, CA: Pacific Press Publishing Association, 1948), p. 164.

5. __________, *Desire of Ages*, (Mountain View, CA: Pacific Press Publishing Association, 1940), p.19.

6. __________, *Desire of Ages*, (Mountain View, CA: Pacific Press Publishing Association, 1940), p. 607.

7. Ellen G. White, *Steps to Christ*, (Phoenix, Arizona: Inspiration Books, 1971), p. 59.

8. Ellen G. White, *Education*, (Mountain View, CA: Pacific Press Publishing Association, 1952), p. 925.

9. Tonne as quoted by Julieta Cabbab and Mark Anthony Cabbab, *Speech Com Manual*, (Manila Bookmark, 1984) p. 65.

10. Frank Mihalic, The *Next 500 Stories*, (Manila: Divine Word Publication Inc., 1989), p. 7.

11. Ellen G. White, *Signs of the Times*, December 25, 1901, par. 11.

12. Ellen G. White, *Testimonies to the Church Vol. 2*, (Mountain View, CA: Pacific Press Publishing Association, 1948), p. 551.

13. __________, *Ministry of Healing*, (Washington D.C.: Review and Herald Publishing Association, 1905), p. 469.

14. __________, *Testimonies to the Church Vol. 6*, (Mountain View, CA: Pacific Press Publishing Association, 1948), p. 277.

15. __________, *Desire of Ages*, (Mountain View, CA: Pacific Press Publishing Association, 1940), p. 113.

16. Wayne Rice, *Hot Illustrations for Youth Talks*, (El Cajon CA: Youth Specialties, 1994), p. 24.

17. Ellen G. White, *This Day with God*, (Washington, D.C.: Review and Herald Publishing Association, 1979), p. 51.

18. Ellen G. White, *Testimonies to the Church Vol.2*, (Mountain View, CA: Pacific Press Publishing Association, 1948), p. 135.

19. Frank F. Mihalic, 1000 Stories You Can Use, Vol. 2 (Manila: Divine Word Publication Inc., 1989), p. 87.

20. Ellen G. White, *Testimonies to the Church Vol. 3*, (Mountain View, CA: Pacific Press Publishing Association, 1948), p. 527.

21. __________, *Testimonies to the Church Vol. 4*, (Mountain View, CA: Pacific Press Publishing Association, 1948), p. 124.

22. __________, *Last Days Events*, (Manila: Philippine Publishing House, 1999), p. 135.

23. Frank F. Mihalic, 1000 Stories You Can Use, Vol. 2, (Manila: Divine Word Publication Inc., 1989), p. 87.

Marvin Marcelino

24. Ellen G. White, *Testimonies to the Church Vol. 8*, (Mountain View, CA: Pacific Press Publishing Association, 1948), p. 242-243.

25. Frank F. Mihalic, *1000 Stories You Can Use, Vol. 2*, (Manila: Divine Word Publication Inc., 1989), p. 87.

26. . __________, *The Next 500 Stories*, (Manila: Divine Word Publication Inc., 1994), p. 30.

27. __________, *Desire of Ages*, (Mountain View, CA: Pacific Press Publishing Association, 1940), p. 550.

28. Ellen G. White, *Selected Messages Vol. 2*, (Washington D.C.: Review and Herald Publishing Association, 1958), p. 187.

29. Frank F. Mihalic, *1000 Stories You Can Use, Vol. 2*, (Manila: Divine Word Publication Inc., 1989), p. 64.

30. Ellen G. White, *Thoughts from the Mount of Blessing*, (Mountain View, CA: Pacific Press Publishing Association, 1996), p. 23

31. Ellen G. White, *Ministry of Healing*, (Washington D.C.: Review and Herald Publishing Association, 1905), p. 360.

32. __________, *Counsels to Parents and Teachers and Students*, (Washington D.C.: EGW Publications, 1913), p. 340.

33. __________, *Christ Object Lessons*, (Washington D.C.: Review and Herald Publishing Association, 1900), p. 386.

34. Ellen G. White, *Testimonies to the Church Vol. 5*, (Mountain View, CA: Pacific Press Publishing Association, 1948), p. 168.

35. __________, *Steps to Christ*, (Phoenix, Arizona: Inspiration Books, 1971), p. 84.

36. Frank F. Mihalic, *1000 Stories You Can Use, Vol. 2,* (Manila: Divine Word Publication Inc., 1989), p. 64.

37. Ellen G. White, *Testimonies to the Church Vol. 5,* (Mountain View, CA: Pacific Press Publishing Association, 1948), p. 170.

38. __________, *Christ Object Lessons,* (Washington D.C.: Review and Herald Publishing Association, 1900), p. 251.

39. __________, *Testimonies to the Church Vol. 5,* (Mountain View, CA: Pacific Press Publishing Association, 1948), p. 639.

40. __________, *Reflecting Christ,* (Hagerstown, MD: Review and Herald Publishing Association, 1985), p. 366.

41. __________, *Testimonies to the Church Vol. 5,* (Mountain View, CA: Pacific Press Publishing Association, 1948), p. 177.

42. Ellen G. White, *SDA Bible Commentary Vol. 6,* (Washington D.C.: Review and Herald Publishing Association, 1978), p. 1105.

43. __________, *Reflecting Christ,* (Hagerstown, MD: Review and Herald Publishing Association, 1985), p. 70.

44. __________, *Desire of Ages,* (Mountain View, CA: Pacific Press Publishing Association, 1940), p. 505.

45. Frank F. Mihalic, *1000 Stories You Can Use, Vol. 2,* (Manila: Divine Word Publication Inc., 1989).

46. Ellen G. White, *Testimonies to the Church Vol. 5,* (Mountain View, CA: Pacific Press Publishing Association, 1948), p. 136.

47. Frank F. Mihalic, *1000 Stories You Can Use, Vol. 2,* (Manila: Divine Word Publication Inc., 1989).

48. Ellen G. White, Review *and Herald*, April 9, 1895, par. 3.

49. Ellen G. White, *SDA Bible Commentary Vol. 5*, (Washington D.C.: Review and Herald Publishing Association, 1978), p. 1140.

50. Ellen G. White, *Signs of the Times*, January 18, 1880, par. 8.

51. Frank F. Mihalic, *1000 Stories You Can Use, Vol. 1*, (Manila: Divine Word Publication Inc., 1989),

52. _________, *Ye Shall Receive Power*, (Hagerstown, MD: Review and Herald Publishing Association, 1995), p. 74.

53. Ellen G. White, *Thoughts from the Mount of Blessing*. (Mountain View, CA: Pacific Press Publishing Association, 1996), p. 15.

54. _________, *Testimonies to the Church Vol. 9*, (Mountain View, CA: Pacific Press Publishing Association, 1948), p. 189.

55. _________, *Lift Him Up*, (Mountain View, CA.: Pacific Press Publishing Association, 1988), p. 293.

56. _________, *Desire of Ages*, (Mountain View, CA: Pacific Press Publishing Association, 1940), p. 644.

57. Frank F. Mihalic, *1000 Stories You Can Use, Vol. 1*, (Manila: Divine Word Publication Inc., 1989).

58. Ellen G. White, *Medical Ministry*, (Washington D.C.: Review and Herald Publishing Association, 1963), p. 316.

59. *Seventh Day Adventist Bible Commentary Vol. 7*, (Washington D.C.: Review and Herald Publishing Association, 1978). p. 934.

Bibliography

1. Beattie, Melody., *Codependent No More*. Minnesota: Hazelden Foundation, 1992.

2. Buscaglia, Leo., Living, *Loving and Learning*. New York: Ballantine Books Inc., 1985.

3. __________. *Loving Each Other*. New Jersey. Slack Inc., 1984.

4. Cabbab Juliet and Cabbab, Mark Anthony., *Speech Com Manual*, Manila Bookmark, 1984.

5. de Chavez, Delba. *Learning is Fun So Is Teaching*. San Pablo City, 1999.

6. Davidoff, Henry., ed. *The Pocket Book of Quotations*. N.Y.: Pocket Books, Simon Schuster Inc., 1994.

7. De Ville, Jard., The *Pastor's Handbook on Interpersonal Relationships*. Maryland: Review and Herald Graphics, 1995.

8. *Familiar Quotations*. Ottenheimer Publisher Inc., 1962; reprint ed., Caloocan City: National Bookstore, 1970.

9. Gothard, Bill. *Institute of Basic Youth Conflicts*. USA. n p., 1981.

10. Mihalic, Frank F., 500 *Stories You Can Use*. Manila: Divine Word Publication Inc., 1993.

11. __________. *1000 Stories You Can Use, Vol. 1 and 2*. Manila: Divine Word Publication Inc., 1989.

12. Morgan, J. S. and Philp, J. R., *You can t Manage Alone*. Michigan: Zondervan, 1985.

13. Morris, Charles, and Eric. Christian Counselor as a Leader Vol. 1. Puan Davao: Philbest, 1987.

14. Morrison, James., ed. *Masterpieces of Religious Verses*. N.Y.: Harper and Row Publication, 1817.

15. *Our Daily Bread Vol. 1*. Michigan: Discovery House Publisher, 1993.

16. __________.   *Vol. 2*. Michigan: Discovery House Publisher, 1995.

17. __________. Vol. 6 Michigan: Discovery House Publisher, 1997.

18. Pollit, R. and Wiltse, V., Helen *Steiner Rice, Ambassador of Sunshine*. NY: Baker Book House, 1994.

19. Pritchard, Ray. *Man of Honor*. Wheaton, Ill: Crossway Books, 1996.

20. Rice, Wayne., Hot *Illustrations for Youth Talks*, El Cajon CA: Youth Specialties. 1994.

21. Sanders, Oswald. *Spiritual Leadership*. Chicago, Ill: Moody Press, 1980.

22. Sala, Harold. *Winning Your Inner Struggles*. Manila: OMF Literature Inc., 1988.

23. Sell, Charles and Virginia Sell. *Spiritual Intimacy for Couples*. Wheaton, Ill. Crossway Books, 1996.

24. *Seventh Day Adventist Bible Commentary 10 Volumes*. Washington D.C.: Review and Herald Publishing Association, 1978.

25. Tucker, James A. and Tucker, Priscilla. *Glimpse of God's Love.* Washington D.C.: Review and Herald Publishing Association, 1883.

26. White, Ellen G. *Acts of the Apostles.* Mountain View, CA.: Pacific Press Publishing Association. 1911.

27. __________. *Child Guidance.* Washington D.C.: Review and Herald Publishing Association, 1954.

28. __________. *Christ's Object Lessons.* Washington D.C.: EGW Publications, 1941.

29. __________. *Counsels to Parents and Teachers and Students.* Washington D.C.: EGW Publications, 1943.

30. __________. *Counsels to Stewardship.* Washington D.C.: EGW Publications, 1940.

31. __________. *Desire of Ages.* Mountain View, CA: Pacific Press Publishing Association, 1940.

32. __________. *Education,* Mountain View, CA: Pacific Press Publishing Association, 1952.

33. __________. *Evangelism.* Mountain View, CA.: Pacific Press Publishing Association, 1970.

34. __________, The *Faith I Live By.* Washington, D.C.: Review and Herald Publishing Association, 1973

35. __________, God's *Amazing Grace.* Washington, D.C.: Review and Herald Publishing Association, 1973.

36. __________. *Gospel Workers.* Washington D.C.: Review and Herald Publishing Association, 1948.

Marvin Marcelino

37. ________, The *Great Controversy Between Christ and Satan*. Mountain View, CA: Pacific Press Publishing Association. 1888.

38. ________. *Last Days Events*. Manila: Philippine Publishing House, 1999.

39. ________, *Lift Him Up*. Hagerstown, MD: Review and Herald Publishing Association, 1988.

40. ________, Maranatha; *The Lord Is Coming*. Washington, D.C.: Review and Herald Publishing Association, 1976.

41. ________, Medical *Ministry*. Mountain View, CA: Pacific Press Publishing Association, 1963.

42. ________. *Messages to Young People*. Nashville, Tennessee: Southern Publishing Association, 1950.

43. ________. *Ministry of Healing*. Mountain View, CA: Pacific Press Publishing Association, 1942.

44. ________, My *Life Today*. Washington, D.C.: Review and Herald Publishing Association, 1952.

45. ________, Our *High Calling*. Washington, D.C.: Review and Herald Publishing Association, 1961

46. ________, Pastoral *Ministry*. Silver Spring, MD: General Conference Ministerial Association, 1995.

47. ________. *Patriarchs and Prophets*. Washington D.C.: Review and Herald Publishing Association, 1958.

48. ________, Reflecting *Christ*. Hagerstown, MD: Review and Herald Publishing Association, 1985

49. __________. *Selected Messages Volume 2*. (Washington D.C.: Review and Herald Publishing Association, 1958.

50. __________. *Steps to Christ*. Phoenix, Arizona: Inspiration Books, 1971.

51. __________, Sons *and Daughters of God*. Washington, D.C.: Review and Herald Publishing Association, 1955.

52. __________, Spiritual Gifts. 4 vols. Battle Creek, MI: Seventh-day Adventist Publishing Association, 1945.

53. __________. *Testimonies for the Church. 9 vols.* 1855-1909. Mountain View, CA: Pacific Press Publishing Association, 1948.

54. __________. *The Master's Immortal Sermons*. Mountain View, CA: Pacific Press Publishing Association, 1971.

55. __________, *The Seventh-day Adventist Bible Commentary*: Ellen G. White Comments. 7 vols. Washington, D.C.: Review and Herald Publishing Association, 1970.

56. __________, The *Sanctified Life*. Washington, D.C.: Review and Herald Publishing Association, 1956.

57. __________, This *Day with God*. Washington, D.C.: Review and Herald Publishing Association, 1979.

58. __________, Thoughts *From the Mount of Blessing*. Mountain View, CA: Pacific Press Publishing Association, 1955.

59. __________, The *Upward Look*. Washington, D.C.: Review and Herald Publishing Association, 1982.

60. __________, The *Review and Herald*

61. _________, The *Signs of the Times*

62. _________, Welfare Ministry. Washington, D.C.: Review and Herald Publishing Association, 1952.

63. _________, *Ye Shall Receive Power.* Hagerstown, MD: Review and Herald Publishing Association, 1995.

64. *With God Nothing Is impossible.* New York: Bantam Books, 1988.

Other Books by Marvin Marcelino

Path to Writing Spiritual Journal Volumes 1-8

101 Objects to Nurture Spirituality

Prepared for Life

SPEAK ENGLISH: Simple Progressive English Achievement Kit
Mastery of Vowels

SPEAK ENGLISH: Simple Progressive English Achievement Kit
Mastery of Consonants

One Anothering: A Biblical Guide to a Better Christian Interpersonal
Relations Volumes 1 & 2

Spiritual Interactive Learning Activities for the Youth

Spirituality versus Religiosity: What Works and What Saves

Take Off Thy Shoes: The Biblical Sanctuary Made Easy

Points of Argument: How to Detect Fallacy

I Am Wonderfully and Chemically Made

I Am Horribly and Chemically Fed

101 Sips of Life's Lessons

www.ingramcontent.com/pod-product-compliance
Lightning Source LLC
LaVergne TN
LVHW020746200726
843506LV00009B/900